# About the Author

John Snyder has a master's degree in history from the University of Cincinnati and a passion for baseball. He has authored more than fifteen books on baseball, soccer, hockey, tennis, football, basketball and travel. He lives in Cincinnati.

# Welcome to the Oddball Series, Red Sox fans.

Here you'll find a wide assortment of the oddest players and moments—wild, weird, wacky, sometimes even wonderful—in team history. In fact, you'll find one for every day of the year.

Not just a round-up of the stories that have been told over and over, this Oddball history by SABR Research Award–winning author John Snyder digs deep into Red Sox history to give you a daily dose of fresh tales you probably haven't heard before.

Take, for example, April 22, 1946, when hometowner Eddie Pellagrini homered in his first at-bat for the Sox. Lucky Eddie loved the number 13. He wore it while playing with three other teams, was born on March 13, and married a woman born on the 13th. He always signed his contract on the 13th of the month. He finished his career with 13 triples and 13 stolen bases and was hit by pitches 13 times.

Tom Oliver was less lucky. In a four-year career, all with the Sox, Oliver batted 1,931 times without hitting a home run—the most at-bats in the modern era without a dinger. Raise a toast to poor Tom, who played his final game on September 23, 1933.

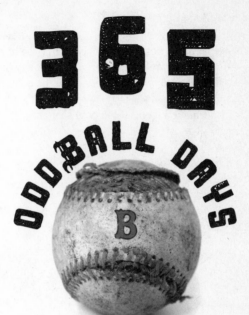

# 365

# ODDBALL DAYS

## IN

# RED SOX HISTORY

JOHN SNYDER

CLERISY PRESS

For further information, contact the publisher at:

 Clerisy Press
1700 Madison Road
Cincinnati, OH 45206
www.clerisypress.com

Library of Congress Cataloging-in-Publication Data

Snyder, John, 1951–
    365 oddball days in Boston Red Sox history / John Snyder.
        p. cm.
    ISBN-13: 978-1-57860-344-2
    ISBN-10: 1-57860-344-7

    1. Boston Red Sox (Baseball team)—History.  I. Title. II. Title:
Three hundred and sixty five days in Boston Red Sox history.

GV875.B62S675 2009
796.357'640974461–dc22

                                              2008053993

Edited by Jack Heffron
Cover designed by Stephen Sullivan
Interior designed by Scott McGrew
Distributed by Publishers Group West

On May 3, 1994, the Sox lost two pitchers in a single at-bat. While pitching to Seattle's Eric Anthony, Frank Viola injured his elbow and had to leave the game. Reliever Paul Quantrill threw a high-and-tight pitch to Anthony, who walked, but charged the mound, sparking a brawl, during which Quantrill injured his finger and had to leave the game. Enjoy the oddest history of the Red Sox ever written.

Jack Heffron, series editor

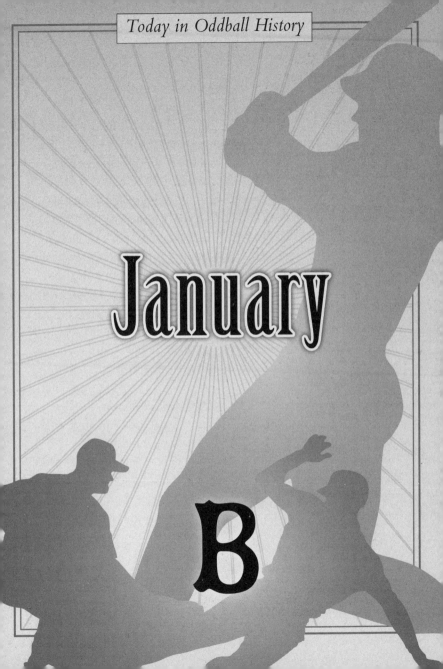

# January

# B

# 01
## January

**T**he question of the day.
What is a Red Sox?
For the purposes of simplicity and consistency, Boston's major league baseball team, which began play in 1901, is called the "Red Sox" throughout this book, though the present-day Red Sox from 1901 through 1907 were most often called the "Americans" by the newspapers of the day. Sometimes the club was also called the "Pilgrims," the "Puritans," the "Plymouth Rocks," or the "Somersets"—this last name a reference to original team owner Charles Somers. None of these nicknames caught the fancy of the Boston baseball fans. The name Boston Americans, chosen because of the franchise's presence in the American League, satisfied nearly everyone but pleased few. It was too generic and failed to identify the club as a Boston institution. Owner John I. Taylor stepped into the breach and called his team the Red Sox, which was actually initiated by another Boston team. The present-day Atlanta Braves originated in Boston as a club in the National Association in 1871 and joined the new National League in 1876. That team was called the Red Stockings because of their bright red hosiery. The nickname passed out of use over time, but Taylor revived it, shortening Red Stockings to Red Sox. The new name immediately gained acceptance with the club's devoted legion of fans.

# 02 January

**T**he question of the day. What is the smallest crowd ever to attend a game at Fenway Park?

The Red Sox have sold out every home game since 2003, and it's difficult to believe that as recently as the 1960s, crowds at the ballpark numbered in the hundreds. Daily attendance records have been kept since 1940, and the smallest "crowd" since that time was on October 1, 1964, when the Sox drew a mere 306 for a game against the Indians.

The following is a list of the 10 smallest known crowds at Fenway Park.

| Date | Opponent | Attendance |
|------|----------|-----------|
| October 1, 1964 | Cleveland | 306 |
| September 29, 1965 | California | 409 |
| September 25, 1965 | California | 461 |
| September 26, 1966 | Washington | 485 |
| September 24, 1963 | Kansas City | 674 |
| September 27, 1943 | Kansas City | 714 |
| September 24, 1943 | Chicago | 822 |
| September 25, 1963 | Kansas City | 909 |
| September 30, 1964 | Cleveland | 934 |
| September 14, 1966 | Chicago | 1,003 |

# 03
## January

**T**he question of the day.

Who hit the first grand slam home run in Red Sox history? Shortstop Freddie Parent hit the first Sox grand slam in dramatic fashion on June 28, 1901. The Red Sox were trailing the Senators 5-2 in the eighth inning in Washington when Parent hit one out of the park facing pitcher Bill Carrick for a 6-5 victory. A native of Biddeford, Maine, Parent played for the Sox from 1901 through 1907 and appeared in baseball's first World Series in 1903 against the Pittsburgh Pirates. He was also the last survivor of that series from either team. Parent died at the age of 96 in 1972.

**04**
January

**T**he question of the day.
Who pitched the first shutout in Red Sox history?

In a game that began in a freak late-spring snowstorm, Ted Lewis pitched the first shutout in Red Sox history, defeating the Indians 5-0 in Cleveland on May 25, 1901. Born on Christmas Day in Machynlleth, Wales, in 1892, Lewis later coached baseball at Harvard, Columbia and Williams. He served as president of Massachusetts State College in 1926 and 1927 and at the University of New Hampshire from 1927 until his death in 1936.

# 05
## January

**O**n this date in 1920, the Red Sox announced the sale of Babe Ruth to the Yankees. Club owner Harry Frazee shipped Ruth to Gotham for $125,000 and a $300,000 loan using Fenway Park as collateral. Frazee was in a precarious financial position because several of the plays in which he invested flopped on Broadway, and attendance at Red Sox games was in decline. Ruth hit a then-record 29 home runs in 1919 and insisted he wouldn't play for the Sox in 1920 unless his salary was raised from $10,000 to $20,000. Frazee was already upset by what he considered to be Ruth's eccentric and immature behavior and believed the salary demands were outrageous. Editorial comments in the 11 newspapers then operating in Boston were split about evenly over the sale of Ruth. It was soon obvious that the sale was a major miscalculation when Ruth hit 54 homers in 1920 and was baseball's best player, as well as the sport's top box office attraction. In what became known as "The Curse of the Bambino," the Red Sox failed to win a World Series between 1918 and 2004. The Yankees, a club that had never appeared in a Fall Classic prior to 1921, captured 26 world championships during that interval.

**B**

**06 January**

**T**he question of the day.
Would Babe Ruth have made it to the Hall of Fame if he had remained a pitcher?

Many baseball historians have speculated that Ruth would have reached the Hall of Fame as a pitcher even if he had never quit the mound to become a full-time batter. The scenario is highly unlikely, however, even though the Babe had a 94-46 record as a pitcher with a 2.28 ERA. Ruth pitched 868 innings between his 20th and 23rd birthdays, including 650 innings in 1916 and 1917. Historically, pitchers who have been used that often that young have had short careers. It's probable that at the time Ruth moved to the outfield in May 1918, a major arm injury was lurking just around the corner. If so, Ruth certainly would have been converted into a first baseman or outfielder at the time his arm was unable to withstand the rigors of pitching. In 1918, the Indians were making a similar move with dead-armed ex-Red Sox star Smoky Joe Wood, an inferior hitter to Ruth. Through his first four seasons in the majors, in which he was strictly a pitcher, Ruth had 361 at-bats, a .299 batting average, nine homers and a .474 slugging percentage. The American League averages during the period were a batting average of .248 and a slugging percentage of .323.

**B**

# 07
## January

**H**appy Birthday Tony Conigliaro. Born this day in 1945, Tony Conigliaro's life reads like a work of fiction. In 1964, at 19, on the first pitch of his first at-bat in his first game at Fenway Park, he hit a home run. By the end of the season, he had 24 homers, the most ever by a teenager. With ambitions of moonlighting as a rock 'n' roll singer, Tony signed a recording contract. In 1965, Conigliaro led the AL in home runs with 32 and hit 28 more in 1966. But he liked to take a stance as close to the plate as the rules permitted, and for that he paid a price. In the 39 months between May 1964 and August 1967, Conigliaro suffered five broken bones from being hit by pitches. The fifth one nearly killed him when he was struck in the face by a pitch from Jack Hamilton of the Angels on August 18, 1967. With his eyesight adversely affected, Tony didn't play again until 1969 and retired in July 1971, with the exception of a 21-game comeback in 1975. After his playing career ended, he founed work in television. Tragedy continued to haunt Conigliaro. He suffered a massive heart attack on January 9, 1982, and never recovered. He had just been hired to work as a color commentator on Red Sox telecasts. Conigliaro needed around-the-clock nursing care until he died of kidney failure on February 24, 1990, at 45.

**08**
**January**

**T**he question of the day.
How many sitting Presidents have seen the Red Sox play?

Ten different sitting Presidents of the United States have seen the Red Sox play a total of 24 games in person. They are William Howard Taft (two games in 1909 and 1911), Woodrow Wilson (five games in 1913 and 1915), Warren Harding (one in 1921), Calvin Coolidge (two in 1927 and 1928), Herbert Hoover (two in 1930 and 1932), Franklin Roosevelt (two in 1934 and 1940), Harry Truman (four in 1946, 1949 and 1952), Dwight Eisenhower (four in 1958, 1959 and 1960), Lyndon Johnson (one in 1965) and George H. W. Bush (one in 1989). Every President from Taft through Johnson saw the Sox play at least once with the exception of Boston native John Kennedy. Twenty-two of the 24 games were played against the Senators in Washington. The other two were on October 9, 1915, when Woodrow Wilson attended the second game of the Red Sox-Phillies World Series at Baker Bowl in Philadelphia, and April 3, 1989, when George H. W. Bush saw the Sox play the Orioles in Baltimore. No President has attended a game at Fenway Park while in office.

# 09
## January

**O**n this date in 1952, the Marines called Ted Williams to active duty to serve as a captain in the Korean War. He was ordered to report to the Willow Grove Naval Reserve Base near Philadelphia on May 2, pending a physical. Williams served three years during World War II but saw no combat. He was a flying instructor at Chapel Hill, North Carolina, Pensacola, Florida and Pearl Harbor. Williams started the 1952 season with the Red Sox and played his last game on April 30. In Korea, he participated in 39 missions as a pilot and didn't return to baseball until August 1953. Ted Williams and Bob Kennedy are the only players to have their major league careers interrupted by both World War II and the Korea War. Jerry Coleman also served in both wars, although he didn't reach the majors until after the end of World War II. Kennedy and Coleman, like Williams, were Marine pilots.

**10**
**January**

**T**he question of the day.

What was Julia Child's opinion of the food at Fenway Park?

In August 1979, a Boston newspaper sent television chef Julia Child to critique the food served at Fenway Park. She didn't like the taste of the famous Fenway Frank. "I do love a good hot dog, but I was disappointed," she said. "A most ordinary frank, rather thin and pale, and a squashy bun with no butter, no relish, just the squirt of ballpark mustard." The french fries were "not bad if you like 'em limp. McDonald's still holds its own there with good french fries." Mrs. Child handed out good marks for the popcorn, which was "good, fresh and crisp." The beer was "very good indeed."

**B**

# 11
## January

**T**he question of the day.

What was Morgan Magic? Joe Morgan replaced John McNamara as manager of the Red Sox on July 14, 1988, with the club holding a 43-42 record. A native of Walpole, Massachusetts, in suburban Boston and a graduate of Boston College, Morgan was 57 years old and had been the Sox third-base coach since 1988. To supplement his income during the off-season, Morgan drove a snow plow, served as a census taker, a toll taker, a substitute teacher, a truck driver and a debt collector. He was a man who received little respect prior to his hiring as manager. He regularly received autograph requests from fans wanting the signature of Hall of Fame second baseman Joe Morgan. The 1988 Red Sox media guide had Morgan's biography accompanied by a photo of fellow coach Rex Slider. At first, Morgan was named interim manager, but the designation was made permanent after the Sox made a dramatic turnaround under their new manager, a phenomenon that was dubbed "Morgan Magic." The club won their first 12 games and 19 of their first 20 games under Morgan's direction and overcame a nine-game deficit to win the AL East. The 12-game winning streak was Boston's longest in 40 years. The Sox also won their first 19 home games under Morgan as part of an American League-record 24-game winning streak at Fenway Park.

**B**

**12 January**

**T**he question of the day.
How many pitchers did the
Red Sox use in 1904?

Amazingly, the Red Sox employed only five pitchers during the entire 1904 season. Cy Young pitched 380 innings, Bill Dinneen 335⅔, Jesse Tannehill 281⅔, Norwood Gibson 273 and George Winter 135⅔. The staff recorded a major league-record 148 complete games out of 157 played. There wasn't a single contest all year in which Boston used more than two pitchers. The hitters were also durable. First baseman Candy LaChance, center fielder Chick Stahl and right fielder Buck Freeman played in every game, while third baseman Jimmy Collins and second baseman Hobe Ferris missed only one game, and shortstop Freddy Parent was absent for only two.

**B**

# 13
## January

**F**ormer Red Sox manager Joe Mc-Carthy died on this date in 1978 at the age of 90. He was hired on September 29, 1947, replacing Joe Cronin, who was promoted to general manager. Although he never played a single game in the majors, McCarthy is one of the most successful managers in the big-leagues. He guided the Cubs from 1926 through 1930. After taking an eighth-place team to fourth in his first season, McCarthy won the NL pennant in 1929 before losing the World Series to the Athletics. He was fired by impatient owner William Wrigley, Jr., late in the 1930 season and was hired by the Yankees. From 1931 through 1946, McCarthy guided the Yanks to eight AL pennants and seven world championships. McCarthy resigned as Yankee manager in May 1946, citing ill health. He managed the Red Sox for two full seasons, and each time lost the pennant on the final day. In 1948, the Sox lost a one-game playoff to the Indians to decide the pennant after McCarthy. In 1949, the Sox went into the final two games with a one-game lead over the Yankees, but lost both games at Yankee Stadium to blow another pennant opportunity. McCarthy resigned in June 1950, again citing health reasons. McCarthy was elected to the Hall of Fame in 1957.

**B**

**14**
**January**

**H**appy Birthday Smead Jolley. Smead Jolley, a left fielder with the Red Sox in 1932 and 1933, was born on this date in 1902. At the time Jolley played in Boston, there was an incline in front of the left-field wall at Fenway Park known as "Duffy's Cliff." An excellent hitter with a .305 lifetime batting average, Jolley was hopeless defensively and often had trouble negotiating the obstacle. On July 19, 1932, during a 7-0 loss to the Indians, Jolley ran up the embankment to attempt to catch Wes Ferrell's fly ball, which was short of the hill and the wall. Upon realizing this, Jolley tried to backtrack and tumbled down the hill while Ferrell's fly ball fell for a hit.

# 15
## January

**O**n this date in 1942, President Franklin Roosevelt gave baseball commissioner Kenesaw Landis the go-ahead to play ball despite the nation's involvement in World War II. In his statement, Roosevelt said he believed that the continuation of the sport would be beneficial to the country's morale. Nearly every player of draft age who could pass the military's physical was in the service by 1945, the last year of the war. No team was hit harder by the war than the Red Sox. The 1942 club included such young stars as Ted Williams (age 23), Johnny Pesky (22), Bobby Doerr (24), Dom DiMaggio (25), Tony Lupien (25), Jim Tabor (25), Joe Dobson (25) and Tex Hughson (26). The war prevented Boston from becoming what might have been a baseball dynasty, as most of these great young players spent time in the service. Williams, DiMaggio and Pesky each missed the 1943, 1944 and 1945 seasons; Dobson missed 1944 and 1945, and Doerr and Hughson missed part of 1944 and all of 1945. After a 93-win season in 1942, the Sox won only 68 in 1943, 77 in 1944 and 71 in 1945. When the players returned from the service in 1946, Boston posted 104 victories and won the AL pennant, the only one earned by the club between 1918 and 1967.

**B**

**16 January**

**T**he question of the day.
    When was the Citgo sign erected?

The now-famous Citgo sign was added to the Kenmore Square area in 1965. It sits atop the Boston University bookstore at 660 Beacon Street. The 60-foot by 60-foot double-sided sign, with its two miles of blinking red, white and blue neon tubing, is visible over the left-field wall at Fenway Park. An immediate pop-art hit, the sign inspired one filmmaker to create a short film in 1968 called *Go Go Citgo*, in which the sign did its hypnotic on-and-off routine to music by the Monkees and Ravi Shankar. The sign was turned off during the energy crisis in 1979 and came close to being torn down in 1983. It was saved by its fans, led by Arthur Krim, who was a Cambridge resident, college professor, and member of the Society for Commercial Archeology, which works to preserve urban and roadside Americana such as neon signs, diners and gas stations. Eventually, the Houston-based Citgo Corporation agreed to keep Kenmore Square's illuminated icon plugged in and maintained.

**B**

# 17
## January

**H**appy Birthday Don Zimmer. Don Zimmer was born on this date in 1931. He was the manager of the Red Sox from July 1976 through September 1980. Zimmer replaced Darrell Johnson less than nine months after the end of the 1975 World Series with the club holding a record of 41-45. Zimmer had previously managed the Padres in 1972 and 1973 to a 114-190 record after a playing career as an infielder that lasted from 1954 through 1965. Zimmer was the first manager to guide the Red Sox to three consecutive seasons of 90 wins or more since Bill Carrigan from 1914 through 1916, but Zimmer will be remembered most in Boston for allowing the Yankees to overcome a 14-game deficit in 1978, and for Bill Lee categorizing him as a "gerbil." The match between the crew cut, conservative, no-nonsense Zimmer and the city of Boston seemed to go together like mustard and clam chowder. Disparaged by players and fans alike, he was constantly booed at Fenway Park and received almost no credit for the 411 victories the club recorded while he was manager, but he did receive the bulk of the blame for the 304 defeats. Despite Zimmer's lack of popularity, the Red Sox drew more than two million fans for the first time in 1977 and 2.3 million in 1979.

# 18 January

On this date in 1973, the Red Sox signed Orlando Cepeda, who was released by the Athletics on December 18, 1972. Cepeda was the first player acquired by any major league club with the new designated-hitter rule in mind. The DH was used for the first time during the 1973 season. From his rookie season in 1958 through 1970, Cepeda was one of the best first basemen in baseball while playing for the Giants, Cardinals and Braves. Two surgically repaired knees made it impossible for him to play defense on a regular basis, however, and Cepeda appeared in only 31 games with the Braves and Athletics. He was 35 years old, and many believed his playing days were over when the Sox acquired him, but he had 358 career homers and hit right-handed. If Cepeda was called upon to hit *only,* the club hoped his knee could stand the strain. The gamble paid off, as he batted .289 with 20 homers and 86 RBIs in 550 at-bats in 1973. Cepada became a fan favorite at Fenway Park, but 1973 was his only season with the club. Cepeda was released by the Sox on March 26, 1974, along with Luis Aparicio. Both Cepeda and Aparicio would later be elected to baseball's Hall of Fame.

# 19
## January

**O**n this date in 1991, Roger Clemens and his brother Randy were arrested at Bayou Mama's Swamp Bar in Houston. The incident increased Clemens's reputation for erratic behavior. He had already been suspended for the first five games of the 1991 season because of his ejection from game one of the 1990 ALCS against the Athletics. According to police, the Red Sox pitcher was arrested after he jumped on the back of Houston policemen Louis Olvedo and choked him as the officer tried to arrest Randy during a disturbance at the bar. Clemens was charged with aggravated assault on a police officer and spent 11 hours in jail before making bail. The charges were dropped on January 9, 1992, but Olvedo filed a civil suit against Clemens because of injuries he claimed he suffered during the altercation. This wasn't the only off-the-field incident involving a Red Sox player to make news during the early months of 1991. During spring training, Wade Boggs fell out of a moving pick-up truck driven by his wife. "I'm lucky to be alive," he said. "The back tire just missed running over my head." Boggs walked away with a few cuts and bruises.

**B**

**20 January**

**O**n this date in 1952, the Red Sox school for rookies opened in Sarasota, Florida, with outfield prospect Jimmy Piersall moving to shortstop, a position he had never previously played. Piersall opened the season at shortstop, but the pressure proved to be too much for the high-strung rookie, and he was moved back to the outfield in early June. The switch from the outfield to short and back to the outfield would have an adverse effect on Piersall's mental stability. He believed the Sox were trying to get rid of him, and the inner turmoil resulted in paranoid-schizophrenic tendencies. In July, Piersall was sent to the minors, and within a few weeks was admitted to the Westborough State Hospital in Massachusetts and received shock therapy. Piersall has no memory of the period between January and September 1952. He later wrote a book called *Fear Strikes Out*, co-authored with a Boston sportswriter, about his battle with mental illness. Piersall recovered and played in 151 games in 1953. Even though the opposition and fans rode him unmercilessly, Piersall hit .272. He continued to battle manic depression and some of his bizarre behavior occasionally resurfaced, but Piersall's big-league playing career lasted until 1967. Since then, he has been active as a coach, broadcaster and talk show host.

# 21
## January

**T**he question of the day.

How did Billy Goodman hurt his ribs in 1953?

Second baseman Billy Goodman was injured in a freak accident in the fifth inning of a 7-4 loss to the Yankees at Fenway Park on May 10, 1953. Goodman made a rush for umpire Jim Duffy after disagreeing with a call, and Jimmy Piersall grabbed Goodman and lugged him from the field. As he struggled to break free from Piersall's grasp, Goodman bruised his ribs, which put him out of action for three weeks.

# 22
## January

**T**he Red Sox signed David Ortiz on this date in 2003 following his re-lease by the Twins. The signing of Ortiz has proven to be one of the best transactions in club history. At the time he was acquired, Ortiz was 27 years old and had a .277 career batting average and 58 homers in 1,417 at-bats. In his first five seasons in Boston from 2003 through 2007, Ortiz became a fan favorite by batting .302 with 208 homers and 642 runs batted in. In each of those five seasons, he finished in the top five in the MVP voting, and he made his fifth All-Star team in 2008. Ortiz set a club record for home runs in a season with 54 in 2006. His impact on the club has gone beyond mere statistics, however. Ortiz's game-winning hits, many of them in the postseason, are already part of Red Sox legend.

# 23
## January

**T**he Red Sox traded Albie Pearson and Norm Zauchin to the Senators for Pete Runnels on this date in 1958. In five seasons in Boston as a second baseman and first baseman, Runnels hit .320 and won batting titles in 1960 and 1962. In 1958, he batted .322 and finished second in the league to Ted Williams. The Sox front office never fully appreciated the contributions of Runnels, however. Club management complained that Runnels was inadequate defensively as a second baseman, but he led the AL in total chances per games in 1958 and 1959 and fielding percentage in 1960. He was moved to first base, but the Sox liked their first baseman to be right-handed power hitters and Runnels was a left-handed singles hitter. Despite winning the batting title in 1960, he was on the bench at the start of the 1961 season behind rookie second baseman Chuck Schilling and aging Vic Wertz at first. Runnels nonetheless worked his way into the lineup, hit .317 in 360 at-bats and won another batting title in 1962. The Sox traded Runnels to Houston after the end of the 1962 season.

# 24
## January

**T**he question of the day.
What did Red Sox owner Bob Quinn say about telecasting games in 1931?

The Short-wave and Television Corporation proposed televising games from Fenway Park in June 1931, which brought a sarcastic reply from Sox owner Bob Quinn. "It has rained every Sunday, our club is in last place, and now you want me to let (the fans) see the games at home," said Quinn. "How do you suppose we are going to pay for the players? If you can furnish me a substitute for money, please let me know immediately." At the time, many in the fledging industry were predicting that television would become commonplace within five years, but it wasn't until the late 1940s that stations would begin regular programming. The Red Sox were on Boston television for the first time on June 3, 1948, for a 3-2 win over the St. Louis Browns from Fenway. The contest was telecast over WBZ-TV. The first baseball game shown by the station took place between the Braves and Cardinals on May 21 from Braves Field.

**B**

# 25
## January

**T**he question of the day.

Who was Tom Oliver?

Tom Oliver played four seasons with the Red Sox from 1930 through 1933, and batted 1,931 times without a home run. He holds the modern (since 1900) major league record for most career at-bats without a homer.

The following is a list of Red Sox players with the most at-bats without a home run.

| Player, Position | Years With Red Sox | At-Bats |
| --- | --- | --- |
| Tom Oliver, of | 1930–33 | 1,913 |
| Hal Rhyne, ss | 1929–32 | 1,414 |
| Eddie Foster, inf | 1920–22 | 907 |
| Hick Cady, c | 1912–17 | 803 |
| Johnnie Heving, c | 1924–25, 1928–30 | 792 |
| Roxy Walters, c | 1919–23 | 764 |
| Otto Miller, inf | 1930–32 | 761 |
| Amos Strunk, of | 1918–19 | 597 |
| Mike McNally, inf | 1915–20 | 592 |
| Jose Tartabull, of | 1966–68 | 581 |

# 26
## January

**L**ulu Ortman, recently jilted by Red Sox outfielder Chick Stahl, was arrested on this date on this date in 1902 in Fort Wayne, Indiana, after unsuccessfully attempting to shoot him. Ortman, a 21-year-old stenographer for a lumber company, tipped off a close friend that she intended to shoot Stahl after he ended their relationship. The friend informed the police superintendent of Fort Wayne, who overtook Ortman just as she was drawing her revolver on Stahl. Not only did Stahl refuse to press charges, but he later resumed his love affair with her.

# 27
## January

**T**he question of the day.
What is the longest losing
streak in Red Sox history?
The longest losing streak in franchise history was in 1906 when they lost 20 games. The Red Sox won the American League pennant in 1904 with a record of 95-59, but the roster seemed to age overnight, and the club was 78-74 in 1905. A total collapse took place in 1906 when the Sox sank to 49-105. The 20-game losing streak started on May 1 and ended on May 25 with a 3-0 win over the White Sox in Boston on a two-hitter by Jesse Tannehill. Rookie back-up catcher Bill Peterson drove in all three runs. During the streak, the Sox were outscored 128-53. The 20-game losing streak is tied for the second-longest in American League history and the third-longest in the majors since 1900. The only longer streaks since the dawn of the 20th century are 23 games by the Phillies in 1961 and 21 by the Orioles in 1988.

**B**

**28**
**January**

On this date in 2003, the Red Sox announced the creation of a new section of seats on top of the left-field wall. The seats were built in 10 sections on top of the 37-foot-high, 231-foot-long Green Monster, and sold for $50 each. (In 2008, the Green Monster seats sold for $160 each.) The idea was to add revenue, but there was another motive. "I also think there's a feeling that these seats could be very cool," Red Sox president Larry Lucchino said. "There's something very special about seeing a game at Fenway from that perspective." The seats also eliminated the unsightly netting on top of the wall that had been in place since 1936. "Nobody likes watching a ball go into a net," said Sox chairman Tom Werner. "The thrill of not only accommodating a few hundred people with a great seat but actually having a ball go into a crowd is a much more exciting experience." Above the wall, three rows of countertops were installed with bar stools behind them, another row of standing room, concession stands, and a short back screen to prevent fans from falling. In 2005, the Red Sox added a smaller seating section, dubbed the Nation's Nest, located between the main seating section and the center-field scoreboard.

# 29
## January

**T**he question of the day. What did Red Sox owner John I. Taylor say about the length of games in 1907?

Major league games a century ago rarely lasted longer than two hours, but that was much too long for John I. Taylor, who was on a campaign to speed up the contests during the summer of 1907.

"This year the games have been dragging a trifle too much in both the American and National Leagues," said Taylor, "and it is my intention now to get after the players and the umpires in our league and make them get a move on. There is absolutely no reason why the regular nine-inning game should not be finished inside of one hour and 45 minutes."

# 30
## January

**H**appy Birthday Walt Dropo.
Walt Dropo, a first baseman with the Red Sox from 1949 through 1952, was born on this date in 1923 in Moosup, Connecticut. A three-sport star at the University of Connecticut, the six-foot-five Dropo was drafted by the Providence Steam-rollers in the first round of the 1947 NBA draft and in the ninth round of the NFL draft by the Chicago Bears in 1948. Dropo had an 11-game trial in 1949 and hit .146 without a home run, then started the 1950 season in the minors. The Red Sox called up Dropo from their farm club in Louisville to play first while their regular first baseman Billy Good-man was out of action. Dropo made the most of the opportunity. In his first 73 games after being recalled, through July 19, Dropo hit .355 with 23 homers and 93 RBIs. He was elected the starting first baseman in the 1950 All-Star Game in a vote of the fans. Dropo finished the season with 144 RBIs to tie teammate Vern Stephens for the league lead. Walt also hit .322 and clubbed 34 homers. He suffered a hairline fracture of his right wrist during spring training in 1951, however, which caused a batting slump. Dropo was back in the minors for five weeks during the season and finished with 11 homers, 57 RBIs and a .239 batting average. He lasted in the majors until 1961, but never came close to his 1950 numbers again.

# 31

## January

**H**appy Birthday Jackie Robinson. Jackie Robinson was born on this date in 1919. On April 16, 1945, The Red Sox offered a tryout to Robinson and fellow African-Americans Sam Jethroe and Marvin Williams, each of whom was a star in the Negro Leagues. The Red Sox were under pressure from many directions to employ African-Americans, including civil rights groups, *Boston Daily Record* sportswriter Dave Egan, an advocate of integration, and Boston City Council member Isadore Muchnick. Muchnick threatened to revoke the permit that allowed the Red Sox to play Sunday games at Fenway Park. The tryout was a charade, as the Red Sox had no intention of breaking baseball's color line, which had been in existence since the 1880s. Following the workout, the Sox front office made no attempt to contact Robinson, Jethroe or Williams. The color line was finally broken when Robinson was signed by the Brooklyn Dodgers on October 23, 1945. He played one season for Montreal in the International League before making his major league debut with the Dodgers in 1947. Jethroe played for the Boston Braves from 1950 through 1952. Williams never played in the majors. It would be 1959 before an African-American played in a regular season game for the Red Sox.

**B**

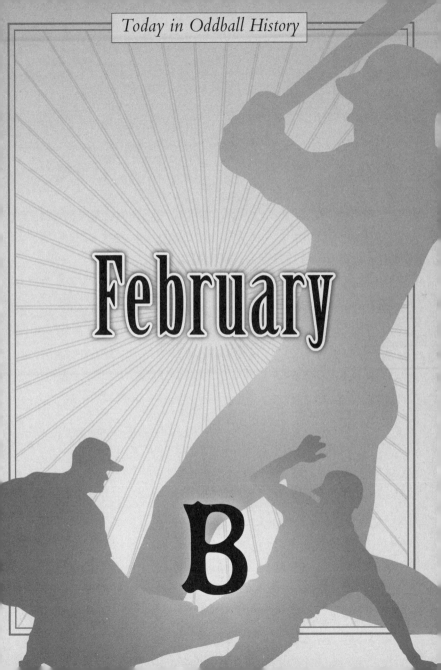

# February

B

# 01
## February

**T**he question of the day. What ironic billboard was posted at Fenway Park in 1950? The Red Sox remained an all-white team until 1959, when Pumpsie Green was added to the roster, but there was a billboard underneath the stands at Fenway Park in 1950 urging fans to "fight for racial and religious understanding." The billboard depicted a white youth holding a bat, standing next to a black youngster, and addressing another white boy. The slogan on the sign read: "What's his race or religion got to do with it—he can pitch." The sign was sponsored by the Massachusetts Committee of Catholics, Protestants and Jews, and by the Red Sox.

# B

**02
February**

**H**appy Birthday Wes Ferrell.
A pitcher with the Red Sox
from 1934 through 1937, Wes
Ferrell was born on this date in 1908.
He was acquired by the Sox in a trade
with the Indians. From 1929 through
1932, he had four consecutive seasons
of 20 or more wins with a cumulative
record of 91-48. But an 11-12 record in
1933 convinced Cleveland he was washed up;
the club had also grown tired of his violent outbursts. Wes's older
brother Rick was the Sox starting catcher, and it was hoped that he
would be a steadying influence. Wes rewarded the Red Sox with
a 14-5 mark in 1934, 25-14 in 1935 and 20-14 in 1936. In addition, he holds the all-time major league record for home runs by
a pitcher with 37. Ferrell also hit one as a pinch-hitter for a total
of 38. He hit 19 of them while wearing a Boston uniform. Ferrell's
seven homers in 1935 are the single-season mark for a Sox hurler.
Wes also hit more homers than his brother Rick in far fewer opportunities, with his 38 in 1,176 at-bats compared to 29 for Rick in
6,028 lifetime at-bats. Rick made the Hall of Fame in 1984. In addition to his batting prowess, Wes posted a 193-128 lifetime pitching
record in addition to six 20-win seasons on clubs seldom in conten-
tion for a pennant. He has long deserved Hall of Fame honors, but
has somehow been ignored.

**B**

# 03
## February

**T**he question of the day.

When did the Red Sox begin playing home games on Sundays? Due to local statutes, the Red Sox couldn't play home games on Sundays until 1929. On February 11 of that year, the Braves received a permit from Boston's city council for games on Sunday in accordance with a recently passed state law that allowed sports to be played on the Christian Sabbath. The law stipulated that the sporting venue couldn't be within 1,000 feet of a church, however, and since that rule applied to Fenway Park, the Red Sox struck a deal with their National League rivals to play 13 Sunday games and three holiday games at Braves Field during the 1929 season. Owner Bob Quinn announced that the Red Sox were also considering abandoning Fenway altogether to play all home games at Braves Field, but he never carried through with the plan. A revision in the law allowed the Red Sox to play Sunday games at Fenway beginning in 1932. While Boston's two major league teams could play on Sunday, the law included a curfew that stipulated that the games must end at precisely 6:30 p.m. Many second games of double-headers in Boston were shortened to six, seven or eight innings because of the law, which remained on the books into the 1950s.

**B**

# 04
## February

**T**he question of the day.

Where was Braves Field?

Braves Field was used by the Boston Braves from 1915 until 1952 when the club moved to Milwaukee. About one-half mile from Fenway Park, it stood on the former site of the Allston Golf Club, the scene of several major golf tournaments before 1914. At the time it opened, Braves Field had the largest seating capacity in baseball at 40,000. The location, however, was far from ideal, as it was on a single streetcar line and hemmed in by railroad tracks and the Charles River. Parking was hopelessly inadequate. The main entrance was on a dead-end street crowded with trucks opposite a busy armory. Unlike most pre-World War I ballparks, there was little intimacy, as most seats were located too far from the field. Boston University purchased Braves Field in 1953. Most of the ballpark was torn down in 1957 and rebuilt as Nickerson Field, where the school's field hockey and soccer teams play today. It was also used by the Patriots from 1960 through 1962 and the Boston Breakers of the USFL in 1983. The virtually unchanged ticket office at Harry Agganis Way and Akimbo Road is now used as a child-care center and a security office for the university. Directly behind the ticket office building is a grandstand that made up part of the right-field bleachers at Braves Field.

**B**

# 05
## February

**R**udy York, a first baseman with the Red Sox in 1946 and 1947, died on this date in 1970. In 1947, York set an unofficial record by starting two hotel fires. On April 26, he fell asleep while smoking in bed. York was dragged to safety by the hotel engineer, who found smoke billowing from beneath the door of York's second-floor room. Unable to arouse York by knocking, he entered with a passkey. The whole room was blazing. As a result of York's negligence, 450 guests at the Miles Standish Hotel in Boston were forced to evacuate. York suffered only slight burns and smoke inhalation. After he was traded to the White Sox on June 14, York started another fire at the Stevens Hotel in Chicago on August 23 by leaving his room with a lit cigarette on a window sill. The drapes and window sash were destroyed before the fire was extinguished. Ironically, one of York's post-playing-career jobs was as a fire prevention officer with the Georgia State Forestry Commission.

**B**

**06
February**

**H**appy Birthday Babe Ruth.
        Born on this date in 1894,
Babe Ruth will be forever known
as a Yankee first and foremost, but
he set his first home-run record and
became a national phenomenon while
still in Boston. Playing for the Red Sox
in 1919, he set the existing single-season
home-run record with 29 in addition to
batting .322 and leading the league in runs
(103), RBIs (114), on-base percentage (.456) and slugging percentage (.657). Prior to 1919, the record for home runs in a season was
27, hit by held by Ned Williamson in 1884 with the present-day
Chicago Cubs. But Williamson hit 25 of his 27 homers at home in
Lakefront Park, which had the smallest outfield in major league
history. In 1919, Ruth hit 20 of his 29 homers on the road. (In six
seasons with the Sox, Ruth hit only 11 of his 49 home runs at Fenway.) The Babe hit four grand slams in 1919, which is still a Red Sox
record. But the most amazing statistic from Ruth's last season with
the Red Sox is that he hit 29 of the club's 33 homers, an unbeliev-
able 88 percent. The only Red Sox players besides Ruth with home
runs were Harry Hooper with three and Snuffy McInnis with one.
Ruth out-homered 10 of the other 15 major league teams in 1919.
The closest individual in the majors to Ruth was the Gavvy Cravath
of the Phillies with 12 home runs.

**B**

# 07
## February

**A**fter sitting out the 1960 season, outfielder Jackie Jensen signed a contact for the upcoming season on this date in 1961. He had announced his retirement on January 26, 1960. Jensen was only 32 but had grown weary of the travel connected with baseball. He hated the long separations from his family, who lived in Nevada, and had a pathological fear of flying. Over the previous six seasons, Jensen drove in 667 runs, the most of anyone in the majors over that period, and was the American League MVP in 1958. It wasn't a smooth return to baseball for Jensen in 1961, as the year away from the sport diminished his skills. He hit .263 with 13 homers and 66 RBIs, left the club for eight days in April, and missed several games because of his fear of flying. Jensen retired from baseball for good at the end of the season. After leaving the game as a player, his wife divorced him and Jensen drifted from one business venture to another, most of which failed, and coached baseball at the University of California, his alma mater, and the University of Virginia. He owned a Christmas tree farm and ran a camp for youngsters in Charlottesville, Virginia, when he died of a heart attack at the age of 55.

**B**

# 08
## February

**T**he question of the day.
Who was the first owner of the Red Sox?

Bostonians, like others around the world, marked the end of the 19th century with parties on December 31, 1900, properly recognizing that the 20th century began on January 1, 1901. (Twenty-first century revelers celebrated the new millennium a year early in 2000.) Among the items discussed throughout Boston during the many New Year's Eve parties in 1900 were rumors that Buffalo's franchise in the American League would be moved to Boston, providing Beantown with two major league teams. The AL publicly acknowledged the fact on January 3. The new Boston team was owned by Charles Somers, who had made his fortune in Cleveland in coal, lumber and shipping in the Great Lakes. The task of placing a new team in Boston was daunting. With the opening of the 1901 season three months away, the club had no ballpark. Nor did they own or lease any land on which to build one. The only player on the Buffalo roster deemed worthy of major league ability was catcher Ossie Schreckengost. In addition, the National League club in Boston was one of the strongest in the older circuit, winning pennants in 1877, 1878, 1883, 1891, 1892, 1893, 1897 and 1898.

**B**

# 09
## February

**T**he question of the day.
How were the Red Sox received in the Boston press in 1901?

Initially, the arrival of the Red Sox wasn't well received. Many newspapermen and fans believed that the city wasn't big enough to support two teams, and the National League Braves were firmly established, having been in the city since 1871. There had been a second Boston club in the Union Association in 1884, the Players League in 1890 and the American Association in 1891. None could turn a profit, and each lasted only a year despite the fact that the Players League and American Association clubs finished the season in first place in their respective leagues. The Red Sox were dubbed the "Invaders" for taking many of the Braves' top stars, including future Hall of Famer Jimmy Collins, with the lure of more lucrative contracts. Many feared that Boston was left with two mediocre teams instead of one good one and predicted the Red Sox were doomed to fail. To attract fans, the Red Sox offered bleacher seats at Huntington Grounds for 25 cents. The cheapest seats at Boston Braves games were 50 cents.

**B**

**10**
**February**

**T**he question of the day.
Which of Boston's two teams
was more successful in 1901?
Once the 1901 season started,
the quality and popularity of the
American League brand of baseball
was apparent, and the writers and fans
changed their tune. The Red Sox finished
in second place with a record of 79-57
and quickly established themselves as Boston's
number-one team. The National League Braves resorted to giving tickets away for free to make their crowds look respectable. In
1901, the Red Sox outdrew the Braves 289,448 to 146,502. The
Sox were also second in the AL in attendance. Boston's celebrated
"Royal Rooters," an organization of noisy and intense fans of Irish
ancestry, shifted their allegiance from the Braves to the Red Sox
in mid-summer. In 1902, the attendance margin between the two
teams in Boston stretched to 3-1 as the Red Sox attracted 348,567
to 116,960 for their NL counterparts in a year in which both teams
finished in third place in their respective leagues. During the 52
seasons that Boston had both an American League and National
League team, the Braves outdrew the Red Sox only seven times
(1921, 1925–26 and 1930–33). In those seven years, the Red Sox
fielded awful teams that averaged 97 losses per year.

**B**

# 11
## February

On this date in 1918, the Red Sox hired 55-year-old Ed Barrow as manager to replace Jack Barry, who enlisted in the Navy. Barrow had previously managed the Tigers in 1903 and 1904, but made his mark as a minor league executive. At the time of his appointment as manager of the Red Sox, Barrow was the president of the International League. Club owner Harry Frazee hired him in part because of his ability to run a club both in the front office and on the field. Because of World War I, military service robbed the Red Sox of several players in 1918. In addition to Barry, who was the starting shortstop in addition to his duties as manager, Duffy Lewis, Hal Janvrin, Del Gainer, Mike McNally, Chick Shorten, Herb Pennock, Jimmy Walsh, Paul Musser and Jimmy Cooney missed the entire year. Dick Hoblitzel, Dutch Leonard, Fred Thomas and Wally Mayer were gone before the season ended. Because of Boston's location on the ocean, most joined the Navy. Despite the handicap, Barrow led the Sox to the world championship in 1918, the last one by the franchise until 2004. Barrow also made one of the most important decisions in baseball history in 1918. In May, he converted pitcher Babe Ruth into an outfielder.

**B**

**12 February**

**H**appy Birthday Dom DiMaggio. Dom DiMaggio was born on this date in 1917. He played center field for the Red Sox from 1940 through 1953, with the exception of three years during World War II (1943–45) when he was in the Navy. DiMaggio batted .298 and among Red Sox players ranks ninth all-time (1,399), seventh in runs (1,099), seventh in doubles (306) and eighth in hits (1,680) and appeared in seven All-Star Games. Dom was the third of three DiMaggio brothers to reach the majors, following Joe and Vince. Overshadowed by his brother Joe, Dom never received the credit he deserved. His unimposing physique contributed to the perception. Because of his glasses and five-foot-nine-inch, 168-pound frame, Dom was nicknamed "The Little Professor." He holds the Red Sox record for the longest hitting streak at 34 games in 1949. It ended on August 9 when he was hitless in four at-bats during a 6-3 win over the Yankees in Boston. Dom hit a sinking line drive in the eighth inning, which his brother Joe caught off of his shoetops. Joe holds the major league record with a hitting streak of 56 games in 1941, but Dom owns two of the three longest streaks in the DiMaggio family. Dom also had a streak of 27 games in 1951. Joe's second-longest streak was 23 games in 1940.

# 13
## February

**O**n this date in 1989, Bucky Dent's "Little Fenway" opened in Delray Beach, Florida. Built to almost the identical scale as the real Fenway (without the 37,000 seats), Dent's mini-Fenway is the centerpiece of his baseball school. The numbers on the Little Fenway scoreboard represent those on October 2, 1978, just prior to Dent's home run, which defeated the Red Sox and contributed to one of the worst days ever for the Red Sox Nation. Mike Torrez, who surrendered Dent's 1978 homer, gleefully participated in the grand opening of Little Fenway, going as far as to pitch to Dent again to christen the park. Dent hit Torrez's fifth pitch onto the screen in left center.

**B**

# 14
## February

**H**appy Birthday Candy LaChance. A first baseman with the Red Sox from 1902 through 1905, Candy LaChance was born on Valentine's Day in 1870. He earned his nickname "Candy" because he preferred peppermints to chewing tobacco. On July 12, 1902, LaChance wrestled Athletics pitcher Rube Waddell before a game in Philadelphia. The wrestling match took place on the field before the first pitch, as curious fans entered the ballpark. Waddell pinned LaChance to the ground and went to the mound to defeat the Red Sox 3-2. LaChance was so exhausted that he asked manager Jimmy Collins to find someone else to play first base, but Collins insisted that he play. He went hitless in four at-bats. LaChance didn't ask out of the lineup often: He led the AL in games played in 1902, 1903 and 1904, and played in every inning of every game in 1903 and 1904.

# 15
## February

**T**he question of the day.
Why did Ted Williams bring a
loaded gun into Fenway Park?
Before the gates opened for a
double-header against the Senators
at Fenway on September 1, 1941, Ted
Williams fired a revolver from behind
the Red Sox bench and shot out the red
globe that covered the first "out" light on
the scoreboard. Shortly after the season ended,
Williams came to Boston to sign his contract for 1942. This time, he
brought two long-range rifles to the ballpark and shot out all of the
lights on the scoreboard. Williams also loved to shoot the many
pigeons that roosted at Fenway Park, a passion he shared with club
owner Tom Yawkey. The activity came to a halt when the Humane
Society got wind of the hunting expeditions inside the ballpark.

**B**

**16
February**

**S**tuffy McInnis, a first baseman with the Red Sox from the world championship season of 1918 through 1921, died on this date in 1960 in Ipswich, Massachusetts. A native of Gloucester, Massachusetts, McInnis hit a bizarre home run at Huntington Grounds in Boston while playing for the Philadelphia Athletics during a 7-3 Red Sox defeat on June 27, 1911. As a timesaving measure, American League president Ban Johnson prohibited warm-up pitches between innings. Sox pitcher Ed Karger threw one anyway, and McInnis leaped into the batter's box and stroked the ball into center field. The Red Sox fielders had not yet taken their positions, and none of them pursued the hit by McInnis, who gleefully rounded the bases. The umpires upheld the home run despite vigorous protests from Red Sox manager Patsy Donovan. It was one of only 20 home runs by McInnis in 7,822 at-bats over 19 major league seasons. He still holds the American League record for the highest fielding percentage by a first baseman in a season. McInnis made only one error in 1921 for a percentage of .9994. He also coached baseball at Harvard from 1949 through 1954.

**B**

# 17
## February

**H**all of Fame pitcher Red Ruffing died on this date in 1986. He pitched for the Red Sox from 1924 through 1930 on some of the worst teams in franchise history and compiled a record of only 39-96. Ruffing holds the all-time Red Sox record for losses in a season when he was 10-25 in 1928; he also posted the second-most defeats with a 9-22 mark in 1929. He was traded to the Yankees on May 6, 1930, just a few days shy of his 26th birthday. With the powerful Yankees, Ruffing thrived, posting 231 wins and 124 losses in New York, where he played in seven World Series. He lasted in the majors until 1947. Ruffing was also the first pitcher to face Ted Williams. It happened on April 20, 1939, as the Sox opened the season with a 2-0 win over the Yanks in New York. In his first at-bat, Williams struck out and finished the day with a double in four at-bats. Williams played right field and batted sixth, behind Doc Cramer, Joe Vosmik, Jimmie Foxx, Joe Cronin and Jim Tabor and ahead of Bobby Doerr, Gene Desautles and Lefty Grove. There were nine future Hall of Famers in the starting lineups of the two clubs. For the Sox were Foxx, Cronin, Williams, Doerr and Grove. For the Yankees were Joe DiMaggio, Lou Gehrig, Bill Dickey and Ruffing.

**B**

**18**
**February**

**H**appy Birthday John Valentin.

An infielder with the Red Sox from 1992 through 2001, Valentin was born on this date in 1967. He is the only player in major league history to pull off an unassisted triple play, hit three home runs in a game and hit for the cycle during his career. The triple play happened while playing shortstop against the Mariners during a 4-3 win in Boston on July 8, 1994. With Seattle runners moving from first and second in the top of the sixth inning, Valentin went to one knee to catch a line drive by Marc Newfield. Valentin then stepped on second to double Mike Blowers and trotted a few steps to tag Keith Mitchell. The Red Sox were trailing 2-0 at the time. In the bottom of the sixth, the Sox scored four times, three of them on Valentin's homer. The game ended when right fielder Wes Chamberlain went over the bullpen wall to take a game-winning home run away from Reggie Jefferson. The contest was also notable because it was the major league debut of Alex Rodriguez, who was only 18 years old and played short for the Mariners. Valentin hit three homers, a double and a single during a ten-inning, 6-5 win over the Mariners at Fenway Park on June 2, 1995. He hit for the cycle on June 6, 1996, during a 7-4 victory over the White Sox in Boston.

**B**

# 19
## February

**I**n a close call during a combat mission over Korea on this date in 1953, Ted Williams escaped without injury when his F-9 Panther jet was hit by enemy fire. Flying with the 33rd Marine Air Group, Williams was one of two hundred pilots in a huge mission aimed at Kyomipo, a troop and supply center 15 miles south of the North Korean capital of Pyongyang. North Korean soldiers hit Williams's plane with small-arms fire, causing it to catch fire and knocking out the landing gear. He turned his crippled jet toward the nearest American air base and crash-landed it on its belly with the flaming aircraft traveling at about 225 miles per hour. The plane skidded for more than a mile before coming to a stop and exploded shortly after Williams exited.

# B

**20 February**

**T**he question of the day. Why did a Boston sportswriter blame automobiles for a poor showing by the Red Sox?

In a column in the August 13, 1914 issue of *The Sporting News*, Tim Murnane blamed automobile ownership as the reason for the substandard play of many of the Red Sox players, including future Hall of Famers Tris Speaker and Harry Hooper. "To my mind, the great cause of the poor work while at home is the automobile craze that has taken hold of the players," Murnane wrote. *The Boston Globe* writer noted that Athletics manager Connie Mack refused to allow his players to drive cars during the season. "Several Red Sox players have machines, including manager Carrigan," continued Murnane, "and the player-speed merchants can be seen flying over Greater Boston speedways night and day, a sure handicap to a ball player's effectiveness."

**B**

# 21
## February

**T**he first black player on the 40-man roster, Pumpsie Green was denied accommodations at the Red Sox spring training headquarters, located at the Safari Hotel in Scottsdale, Arizona, on this date in 1959. Segregation wasn't unusual during spring training in 1959. Most black players lived apart from their white teammates because of Jim Crow policies in both Arizona and Florida. Many were housed either at hotels that catered exclusively to African-Americans or in private residences. The Red Sox, however, could find no place in Scottsdale that would allow Green to stay overnight. The club had to put him up at a hotel in Phoenix 17 miles away that the San Francisco Giants used for their black players and provided Green with a driver to take him back and forth from Phoenix to Scottsdale. Green was sent to the minors before Opening Day, leaving the Red Sox as the only team in the majors with an all-white roster. He became the first African-American to play in a regular season game for the Red Sox when he served as a pinch-runner for Vic Wertz in the eighth inning of a 2-1 loss to the White Sox in Chicago on July 21, 1959. Green played four seasons for the Red Sox and hit .244 with 12 homers in 327 games as an infielder.

**B**

**22**
**February**

**T**he question of the day.
What is the longest game (by innings) in Red Sox history?

The longest game in Red Sox history is 24 innings, played against the Athletics in Boston on September 1, 1906. It is also the second longest in American League history and the fourth longest in the majors. The Sox lost 4-1 before a Saturday afternoon crowd of 18,000. Both Jack Coombs of the A's and Joe Harris of the Sox pitched complete games in a contest that lasted four hours and 47 minutes. Coombs struck out 18, hit a batter, and allowed 14 hits and six walks, while Harris fanned 14 and yielded 16 hits and two walks. The Athletics scored a run in the third inning on two fielding miscues by Harris, and the Red Sox tied the game 1-1 in the sixth. The deadlock remained unbroken for 17 innings as neither pitcher allowed a run from the seventh inning through the 23rd. In the fateful 24th inning, the Athletics had a runner on first with two out when Harris surrendered a single and two triples. Harris's 24 innings are a record for most innings in a game in a defeat, a mark that will likely stand forever. Hailing from the Boston suburb of Melrose, Harris had a horrific 2-21 record in 1906, which included 14 losses in a row. Shortly before the season ended, he contracted typhoid fever. Harris's final career record was 3-30 over three seasons.

**B**

# 23
## February

**T**he question of the day.
When did the Red Sox play
29 innings in one day?

The Red Sox played in the two longest double-headers by innings in American League history, both 29 innings. The first was one July 4, 1905, against the Athletics in Boston. In the opener, played in the morning, Philadelphia won 5-2. In the afternoon, the A's won again 4-2 in 20 innings. Cy Young and Rube Waddell both pitched complete games. Waddell allowed two Boston runs in the first, then pitched 19 consecutive scoreless innings. The A's tied the score 2-2 in the sixth on a homer by Harry Davis. Young issued no walks in the game, but hit John Knight in the head with a pitch in the 20th inning, knocking him unconscious. The hit batsman, along with an error and two singles, produced the two runs that led to the Boston defeat. The Red Sox and Yankees played 29 innings in a twin bill in New York on August 29, 1967. The Sox won the first game 2-1, but lost the second 4-3 in a 20-inning marathon. Ken Harrelson made his Red Sox debut and hit a homer in his first at-bat to give the Sox a 2-0 lead in the second inning. The score was 2-2 after nine innings. Both teams scored in the 11th. In the 20th inning, Horace Clarke singled in the winning run off Jose Santiago.

**B**

**24**
**February**

**T**he question of the day.

Who was Bob Quinn?

The Red Sox had a record of 605-1,081 for a .359 winning percentage from 1922 through 1932, the worst in American League history over 11 consecutive seasons. In an eight-team league, the Red Sox finished last in nine of the 11 campaigns. The only record worse over 11 straight seasons in the majors since 1900 has been 584-1,090 (.349) by the Phillies from 1933 through 1943. Harry Frazee pushed the Red Sox into the abyss by selling the club's top stars, starting with Babe Ruth in 1920. Frazee sold the Red Sox in July 1923, however, to a group headed by Bob Quinn. It was Quinn who drove the Red Sox franchise straight into the ground. The worst club under the Frazee regime was the 1922 outfit with a record of 61-93. Most of Quinn's aggregations fell below the standards of Frazee's depleted teams. The 1932 season was the worst in Red Sox history. The club lost 111 of its 154 games. The season attendance was 182,150, less than what the club drew in the first five home games in 2008. In February 1933, with the nation near the nadir of the Great Depression, Quinn was some $350,000 in debt and sold the Red Sox to Tom Yawkey.

**B**

# 25
## February

**O**n this date in 1933, Tom Yawkey bought the Red Sox at a time when it was the worst franchise in baseball, saving it from financial ruin. His uncle, William Yawkey, owned the Detroit Tigers from 1904 through 1907. William Yawkey was fabulously wealthy. Tom Yawkey's father died when he was very young, and his wealthy uncle took care of him and his mother. After Tom's mother died in 1917, William Yawkey and his wife formally adopted him. Tom Yawkey inherited $40 million on February 21, 1933, his 30th birthday. Four days later he bought the Red Sox from Bob Quinn for $1.5 million. Yawkey owned the Red Sox for 43 years, but despite the millions he threw into the ball club, a world championship eluded him. His teams never lacked superstars or Hall of Fame candidates, but they seldom had the depth or team chemistry necessary to win a pennant. The Sox reached the World Series three times during Yawkey's regime, in 1946, 1967 and 1975, only to lose in the seventh game on each occasion. He also drew considerable criticism for his failure to intregrate the Red Sox until 1959. Despite the problems, Yawkey became a beloved figure in Boston because of his benevolence and generosity.

**B**

# 26
## February

**O**n this date in 1966, African-American pitcher Earl Wilson was refused service at two bars in Winter Haven, Florida, where the Red Sox trained for the first time after eight seasons in Scottsdale, Arizona. Wilson went to one establishment with white teammates Dave Morehead and Dennis Bennett and friend of Bennett's. The four sat at the bar, and Wilson was turned away. The four went to another bar and were stopped at the door. The Red Sox front office wanted to keep the incident out of the newspapers but the story broke, embarrassing the ball club. The Sox publicly expressed outrage and barred players from entering the two businesses that refused to serve Wilson.

B

# 27

## February

**O**n this date in 1942, President Franklin Roosevelt ruled on the draft status of Ted Williams. In January, Williams had been re-classified from 3-A, a designation he received as the sole financial support of his mother, to 1-A, making him eligible for the draft. The decision had been made by Williams's draft board in Princeton, Minnesota, where he spent his winters. Roosevelt changed Williams's draft status back to 3-A, instructing General Lewis Hershey, head of the Selective Service Board, that being eligible for the draft would place "undue hardship" on Williams. Williams received considerable criticism from fans for the change, because many believed he was receiving preferential treatment. A week later, he said that he would enlist as soon as the 1942 baseball season was over. He enlisted as a Navy aviation cadet on May 22 and entered the service in November 1942. Williams served three years in the military during World War II and 14 months during the Korean War in 1952 and 1953.

B

**28**
**February**

**T**he question of the day.
What Indians third baseman
started a game-ending triple play
against the Red Sox with his head?

Odell Hale was the infielder who
started one of the most unusual triple
plays in history on a ball that glanced
off his head during a 5-3 Indians win over
the Red Sox at Fenway Park on September
7, 1935. The bases were loaded in the ninth
inning with none out, Joe Cronin at bat, and Orel Hildebrand
pitching. Cronin hit a vicious line drive that glanced off Hale's
glove, then struck his forehead with such force that it rebounded
to shortstop Billy Knickerbocker, who caught it before it touched
the ground. Knickerbocker threw to Roy Hughes at second base to
force Billy Werber. Hughes whipped the ball to first baseman Hal
Trosky to complete the triple play before Mal Almada could return
to the bag.

**B**

# 29
## February

**T**he question of the day.
Who was bitten in the posterior by his own false teeth?
During a 15-6 loss to the Tigers at
Fenway Park on September 21, 1923,
Red Sox relief pitcher Clarence Blethen
was the unfortunate individual who
was chomped by his own false teeth. He
didn't like to pitch while wearing his false
teeth, believing that he looked more menacing
without them, and kept them in his back pocket. Blethen slid into
second base on a close play, and received a nasty wound when his
choppers clamped down on his buttcoks.

**B**

# March

# B

# 01
## March

**H**al Janvrin, an infielder with the Red Sox from 1911 through 1917, died on this date in 1962. He hit two inside-the-park homers during a farcical 10-9 loss to the Senators on October 4, 1913 in Washington. It was played on the last day of the season. The Senators used eight pitchers, including infielder Germany Schaefer, catcher Eddie Ainsmith, outfielder Joe Gedeon and 43-year-old manager Clark Griffith. Griffith's catcher was 44-year-old coach Jack Ryan, who hadn't donned the catcher's gear in a big-league game in 10 years. The makeshift pitchers contributed to a six-run Red Sox rally in the ninth inning. Hall of Fame pitcher Walter Johnson started the contest in center field, but was forced to take the mound to stem the rally. The game brought out 3,000 cavalry soldiers from a camp in Winchester, Virginia, for "Army Day." Janvrin hit only six homers during a 10-year career in which he played in 756 games and accumulated 2,221 at-bats.

**B**

**02 March**

**H**appy Birthday Moe Berg.
Born on this date in 1902,
Moe Berg played as a catcher for
the Red Sox from 1935 though 1939
at the end of a 15-year major league
career. He may have been the most
intelligent man ever to play professional baseball. Berg read and spoke
12 languages, including Sanskrit. He held
degrees from Princeton University, Columbia
Law School and the Sorbonne. Berg was never more than a reserve
catcher, but he stayed in the majors because of his intelligence and
defensive abilities. Few knew that Berg was also working as a spy
for the United States government during his playing career. At the
end of the 1934 season, just before the Sox acquired him from the
Indians, Berg was added at the last minute to a team of All-Stars,
including Babe Ruth, on a goodwill trip to Japan. Organizers cited
his fluent Japanese as the reason for including him on the roster
of stars. However, instead of playing, Berg spent much of his time
taking photographs of key Japanese military installations from the
roof of a Tokyo hospital. These were later used in American air
raids during World War II. Once the war started, Berg went behind
enemy lines to determine Germany's nuclear potential. Berg's gift
for languages served him well, and he always returned safely.

# 03
## March

On this date in 1932, Red Sox pitcher Ed Morris was stabbed to death at a fish fry in Century, Florida, just over the state line from his home in Flomaton, Alabama. The event was intended as a farewell to Morris on the eve of his departure for spring training in Savannah, Georgia. The party atmosphere was interrupted by an argument between Morris and Joe White, a gasoline attendant from Brewton, Alabama. White knocked Morris down during the altercation, and as the Sox pitcher lay on the ground, White stabbed him. Morris died a few hours later at the hospital. White was twice put on trial for manslaughter, but he was acquitted both times after pleading self-defense.

**B**

**04
March**

**H**appy Birthday Jack Fisher.
Born on this date in 1939,
Jack Fisher gave up a home run
to Ted Williams during Williams's last
big-league plate appearance. It took
place on September 28, 1960, before a
crowd of 10,554 at Fenway Park. Fisher
was pitching for the Orioles and threw
a 1-1 pitch in the eighth inning that Williams drove into the right-field bleachers. It was
Ted's 521st career homer and gave the Sox a 5-4 victory. Williams
took his defensive position in left field at the start of the ninth
and was replaced immediately by Carroll Hardy. Williams left the
field to a standing ovation. After the game, he made the surprising
announcement that he had just played in his last game, bypass-
ing the upcoming three-game series against the Yankees in New
York. Williams was honored in ceremonies prior to the September
28 contest. "Baseball has been the most wonderful thing that has
even happened to me," said Williams, "and if I could do it all over
again, I would want to play for the best owner in the business, Tom
Yawkey, and the greatest fans in America."

# 05
## March

**O**n this date in 1975, Tony Conigliaro signed a minor-league contract with the Red Sox for the upcoming season. Conigliaro was 30 years old and hadn't played since retiring in July 1971 because of vision problems that adversely affected his depth perception following the beaning he suffered on August 18, 1967. His eye difficulties appeared to clear up, which spurred Conigliaro to try another comeback. After a fine spring, he won the starting job as the club's designated hitter by the start of the regular season. On Opening Day, Tony received four standing ovations. Conigliaro's vision failed again, however, and he hit a measly .123 with two home runs in 57 at-bats. The Red Sox sent him to their farm club in Pawtucket in the International League on June 14. Conigliaro played 37 games there and hit just .203 with three homers before retiring on August 21, this time for good. He then went into television and did the sports news for a station in Providence for a year before moving to KGO-TV in San Francisco in 1976.

**06**
**March**

**T**he question of the day.
Who was Deacon McGuire?
Deacon McGuire managed the Red Sox from June 1907 through August 1908. He had a long major league career as a catcher that lasted from 1884 through 1912. McGuire was the first player to appear in 1,500 games as a catcher, a significant achievement in an era in which catchers wore thin gloves with little or no padding and no shinguards. By 1907, McGuire was 43 years old and played in five games over two seasons with Boston, each as a pinch-hitter. He collected hits in three of the at-bats, one of them a home run, for a batting average of .600. McGuire inserted himself into the second game of a double-header on July 25, 1907 at Huntington Grounds and hit a dramatic home run. With Detroit leading 2-1 and two out in the ninth inning, McGuire pinch-hit for Tex Pruett. With two strikes on him, McGuire hit a drive that landed on the steep bank in left field. The ball hopped over the fence, which, according to the rules of the day, was a home run. It was also the first pinch-hit homer in Red Sox history. The Sox lost the game 3-2 in 11 innings, however. When McGuire pinch-hit on August 24, 1908, he became the oldest player in Red Sox history at 44 years, nine months and six days.

# 07
## March

**T**he question of the day.

How many managers did the Red Sox employ in 1907?

The Red Sox went through five managers in less than three months during the 1907 season. The five were Chick Stahl, Cy Young, George Huff, Bob Unglaub and Deacon McGuire. Stahl was the manager at the start of spring training, but tragically committed suicide on March 28. Owner John I. Taylor wanted to become the field manager himself following Stahl's suicide, but AL president Ban Johnson refused to allow it and told Taylor to confine his duties to the front office. Young started the regular season running the club, but made it clear to ownership that he would take the job only on a temporary basis. After six games, Young was replaced by Huff, who was 36 years old and was employed as athletic director at the University of Illinois. Huff managed only eight games with the Sox, losing six of them, and returned to his job at Illinois, a post he held until his death in 1936. Huff was replaced by Unglaub, who was only 26 and the club's starting first baseman. He had a 9-20 record when he was succeeded by McGuire on July 25. Unglaub remained with the Red Sox as a player until the following season when he was traded to the Senators.

**08**
**March**

**T**he question of the day.
Where did the Red Sox conduct spring training during World War II?

The Red Sox trained in Sarasota, Florida, from 1933 through 1942. To save on travel expenses during the Second World War, baseball commissioner Kenesaw Landis ordered teams to train north of the Ohio River and east of the Mississippi River. In 1943, the Sox conducted spring training at Tufts College in Medford, Massachusetts, in both Medford and Baltimore in 1944, and Pleasantville, New Jersey, located near Atlantic City in 1945. The Red Sox returned to Sarasota in 1946. Major league camps that season were unique, as returning veterans competed with war-time fill-ins for spots on the club. The Red Sox' spring training roster included 28 players who spent the entire 1945 season in the military. Many of them, such as Ted Williams, Johnny Pesky, Bobby Doerr, Dom DiMaggio, Tex Hughson, Mickey Harris, Hal Wagner and Joe Dobson, reclaimed their old positions. Wartime players like Bob Johnson, Bob Garbark, Johnny Tobin, Ben Steiner, Pete Fox, Dolph Camilli, Ty LaForest, Pinky Woods and Otie Clark, were released. Of the 35 players who appeared in a game for the Red Sox in 1945, only 11 returned in 1946. Despite the turnover, the Sox won the American League pennant in 1946.

# 09
## March

On this date in 1981, Carlton Fisk signed a contract as a free agent with the White Sox. The Sox lost both Fisk and Fred Lynn through a contract snafu. According to a clause in the Basic Agreement between the players and the owners, a player must be tendered a contract by December 20. If a club failed to do so, a player could declare himself a free agent. Since the envelopes containing their contracts were dated December 22, both Fisk and Lynn were eligible to become free agents, and both exercised the option. Lynn waved his right and was traded to the Angels. The Sox offered Fisk a hefty contract and thought that the money, Carlton's New England ties, and 11 years with the club would be enough to keep him in Boston. Fisk instead signed a deal with the White Sox. In a strange twist, the White Sox were scheduled to play the Red Sox on Opening Day in 1981 on April 10. Fisk hit a three-run homer in the eighth inning to spark his new club to a 5-3 win over his former teammates before 35,124. He played in Chicago for 13 seasons and retired after the 1993 season at the age of 45.

# 10
## March

**P**rior to the first spring training game on this date in 1951, actress Dorothy Lamour threw out the ceremonial first pitch. The Reds defeated the Red Sox 4-0 in Sarasota, Florida. Best-known for her roles in the Bob Hope-Bing Crosby road pictures, Lamour was in town for the location filming of *The Greatest Show on Earth*, which won the 1952 Oscar for best picture.

# 11
## March

**O**n this date in 1971, Rico Petrocelli and the Red Sox were named as co-defendants in a $1 million damage suit charging Petrocelli with assault and battery. The suit was filed on behalf of Susanne Mondlin of Roosevelt, New Jersey, who was a flight attendant with United Air Lines. Mondlin accused Petrocelli of assaulting her on a flight from Boston to Detroit on April 19, 1970. She claimed that he grabbed her "indecently" while she was serving coffee and later scratched her and kicked her. The case was settled out of court.

**12**
**March**

**G**round was broken for the construction of Huntington Grounds, the first ballpark used by the Red Sox, on this date in 1901. It was located on the south side of Huntington Avenue just east of Forsyth Avenue (then known as Rogers Avenue). The left-field fence ran along Huntington and the third base side was on Rogers. It was easily reached by streetcar from downtown Boston, the Back Bay, Roxbury, and Brookline, a necessity in the days before the automobile became commonplace. The land was owned by the New York, New Haven & Hartford Railroad and leased to the Boston Elevated Railway, which operated most of the streetcars in the city. The Red Sox sublet the property from the streetcar company, which had a line on Huntington. The directors of the Boston Elevated reasoned that a ballpark on the line would increase ridership. Before the Red Sox moved in, Huntington Grounds was used for carnivals and traveling shows, and it was on the opposite side of the street from where Buffalo Bill's Wild West Show and the Barnum and Bailey circus played in Boston.

# 13
## March

On this date in 1938, Ted Williams played his first game in a Red Sox uniform. He was acquired by the Red Sox at the age of 19 on December 7, 1937, from the San Diego Padres of the Pacific Coast League for Dom Dallesandro, Al Niemic and $25,000. The Sox outbid the Yankees, Giants, Athletics and Tigers to obtain Williams. He had signed with the minor league Padres at 17, shortly after graduating from San Diego's Hoover High School in 1936. Most scouts considered him to be one of the best prospects in the history of the PCL, but thought he needed at least one more season in the minors to be a productive major leaguer. The Sox concurred and sent Williams to their Minneapolis farm club in the American Association on March 21, 1938. The club didn't need to rush Williams to the majors because of a strong outfield. Ben Chapman batted .340 and collected 40 doubles; Joe Vosmik had a .324 batting average, scored 121 runs, and led the league with 201 hits; and Doc Cramer was second in hits with 198. Williams displayed his vast potential at Minneapolis by batting .361 with 43 homers and 142 RBIs. As a rookie with the Red Sox in 1939, Williams led the AL in runs batted in with 145 in addition to 31 homers, 131 runs scored and a .327 average.

**B**

**14**
**March**

**H**appy Birthday Jack Rothrock.
Born on this date in 1905,
Jack Rothrock played for the
Red Sox from 1925 through 1932. On
September 29, 1928, Sox manager Bill
Carrigan listed Rothrock as a catcher in
the starting lineup against the Indians in
Cleveland so he would have appeared at
all nine fielding positions during the season.
Rothrock was only a catcher on paper, howev-
er, and pitcher Danny MacFayden had a similar status on the lineup
card in left field. In the bottom of the first inning, Rothrock moved
to left field and Joe Heving went into the game as a catcher. Since
Rothrock was listed as a starting catcher on the lineup card, he
received credit for an official game at the position even though he
didn't don the catcher's gear or take a position behind the plate.
The Red Sox won the game 6-5. During the 1928 season, Rothrock
played 40 games at shortstop, 36 at second base, 26 in left field,
19 in right, 17 at third base, 16 at first base, one as a catcher and
one as a pitcher. The pitching performance came on September
24 when Rothrock hurled a perfect inning during an 8-0 loss to the
Tigers in Detroit.

# 15
## March

**T**he question of the day.
What is located today on the former site of Huntington Grounds?

The Red Sox played their first 11 seasons from 1901 through 1911 at Huntington Grounds on the south side of Huntington Avenue east of Forsyth Street. The first modern World Series was played at the ballpark in 1903, and it was the scene of Cy Young's perfect game in 1904. The property was used by the Huntington YMCA from 1916 through 1953 when it was purchased by Northeastern University. Today, the school's Cabot Physical Education Center is located on the site. The building includes a World Series Exhibit Room with memorabilia from the 1901-11 Red Sox teams, and a plaque outside marks where the left-field foul pole stood. There is a full-sized statue of Cy Young where the pitcher's mound used to be (in the Churchill Hall Mall). Sixty feet away, another plaque indicates the location of home plate.

**16 March**

**T**he question of the day.

What were the dimensions of Huntington Grounds?

Today's fans know of the tradition-rich Fenway Park that's so integral to Red Sox lore, but the earliest ballparks were modest affairs, hardly built for the long haul. That was certainly true of Huntington Grounds, home of the club from 1901 through 1911. It had a wood-frame grandstand and bleachers with room for some 9,000 fans. Often, the bleachers were jammed full of bargain hunters while the grandstand was almost empty. The diamond was about 90 feet from the stands, giving players plenty of room to snag foul balls. The dimensions of the field were approximately 350 feet down the left-field line, 440 feet in left-center, a distant 530 feet to straight-away center, and 280 feet to right field. An angle of fencing in right-center was 635 feet from home plate. Despite the distances, the Red Sox hit 216 home runs at Huntington Grounds during the club's 11 seasons there, compared to 109 on the road. During the "Dead Ball Era," larger parks actually meant more home runs. Most homers were inside the park, splitting the gaps between the outfield, allowing the batter to circle the bases while outfielders chased the ball to the distant fences.

**B**

# 17
## March

**O**n this date in 1953, the Red Sox became the only big-league team in New England, as the Braves moved to Milwaukee. Attendance at Braves Field peaked at 1,455,429 in 1948, when the club won the National League pennant, but dropped to 944,381 in 1950, 487,475 in 1951 and 281,278 in 1952. Following the 1952 season, Braves owner Lou Perini considered moving his club to Milwaukee, where he owned a minor league club in the American Association, but he decided to give it a go in Boston for at least one more season. Browns owner Bill Veeck wanted out of St. Louis, however, and had also set his sights on Milwaukee. Perini had the rights to Milwaukee and blocked Veeck's move. This made Perini a villain in Milwaukee because he was denying fans there a major league team. Backed into a corner, he moved the Braves less than a month before the start of the 1953 season. The Braves were an immediate success in Milwaukee, drawing 1,826,397 fans in 1953, then a National League record, and more than two million for five consecutive seasons beginning in 1954. The club also won the NL pennant in 1957 and 1958. Veeck sold the Browns in September 1953 to a Baltimore group, where the club was moved and renamed the Orioles.

**B**

**18 March**

**T**he question of the day.

What were the playing conditions at Huntington Grounds?

The playing field at Huntington Grounds, home of the Red Sox from 1901 through 1911, was far from ideal. Much of the ground consisted of sand where the grass never grew. Center field was so deep (635 feet at one point), that few balls ever reached that far, so the club didn't go to the expense of cutting the hip-high weeds. A toolshed in deep center was in play, and a steep bank led to the left-field fence. Between the 1902 and 1903 seasons, the field sank because of the heavy winter snows and spring thaw and had to be almost completely filled and graded. Players complained that the turf was rocky and uneven. A year later it was plowed up and leveled. The New York, New Haven & Hartford Railroad repair yards bordered the park behind home plate, and the engines of the passing trains and locomotives belched ashes and cinders that drifted into the eyes of the players and fans. In addition, thousands of horses traveled on the streets of Boston during the first decade of the 20th century, leaving piles of manure on the streets. During dry periods, the manure turned to dust under the weight of the many wagons, carriages and trolley cars. The dried manure became airborne on windy days, leading to another nuisance.

# 19
## March

**T**he Red Sox added one of the best pitchers in baseball history to their roster on this date in 1901 with the signing of Cy Young. He had a career record of 286-170 entering the 1901 season, but was 34 years old—the oldest pitcher in either league. Many considered him to be washed up after a 19-19 record with the St. Louis Cardinals in 1900. Young wasted no time burying that notion, however, with a 33-10 record with Boston in 1901 along with a 1.62 ERA, 38 complete games in 41 starts, five shutouts and a league-leading 158 strikeouts. He walked only 37 batters in 371⅓ innings. Young followed that great season with a 32-11 record in 1902, 28-9 in 1903 and 26-16 in 1904. He played eight years for the club. Young finished his career with an all-time record 511 big-league victories. Walter Johnson follows at a distant second with 417. Young is also first in games started (815), first in complete games (749), first in innings pitched (7,355⅔) and fourth in shutouts (76). What is more amazing is that he racked up these stats during a time of change in the game. During his career, the distance from the mound to home plate was increased from 55 feet to 60 feet, six inches. He won during the 1890s when hitters dominated the game and in the "Dead Ball Era" of the early 1900s when pitchers held the advantage.

**20 March**

**O**n this date in 1918, Red Sox players Harry Hooper, Babe Ruth, Everett Scott, Joe Bush and Wally Schang narrowly escaped death in a bizarre cab ride while at spring training in Hot Springs, Arkansas. The players engaged a cab driver to take them from the racetrack to the team's hotel. Halfway to their destination, the cabbie stopped and demanded that he be paid for his services. The players called a policeman, who ordered the driver to take the Sox players where they wanted to go. The driver did so, but at a frightening speed. Tearing around the downtown area, he banged into a bus, knocked down a horse and smashed into a wagon before Hooper threatened to beat him up, finally allowing the players to escape unharmed. Scott holds the record for the longest playing streak in Red Sox history. He played in 832 straight games for the club before he was traded to the Yankees on December 20, 1921. His total streak ended at 1,307 games in 1925. The only streaks longer than Scott's are those of Cal Ripken, Jr. (2,632) and Lou Gehrig (2,130). The only other Red Sox player to appear in at least 500 games in a row is Buck Freeman with 535 from 1901 through 1905.

# 21
## March

**T**he question of the day.

When did the Red Sox set a club record with eight home runs in a game?

The Sox set the record on July 4, 1977, during a 9-6 win over the Blue Jays at Fenway Park. The eight homers were struck in a span of four innings. George Scott got things rolling with a two-run homer in the fifth. The rest were all solo homers. Fred Lynn hit one in the sixth, and Bernie Carbo and Butch Hobson connected for the circuit in the seventh. There were four homers in the eighth, which tied a club mark for most home runs in an inning. Lynn, Jim Rice and Carl Yastrzemski hit back-to-back-to-back homers, and after Carlton Fisk was retired, Scott hit his second home run of the game. It was also the first time that the Blue Jays played at Fenway. The Red Sox hit 83 homers over a 44-game span from May 19 through July 4. The 83 home runs were hit by Scott (16), Rice (14), Yastrzemski (14), Hobson (11), Fisk (nine), Lynn (seven), Carbo (six), Dwight Evans (four), Rick Burleson (one) and Denny Doyle (one). During one stretch in June, the Sox hit 33 homers in 10 games. The Sox set a club record for home runs in a season in 1977 with 213—124 of them struck at Fenway. It stood until the 2003 Red Sox hit 238 home runs.

## B

# 22
## March

**O**n this date in 1972, the Red Sox traded Sparky Lyle to the Yankees for Danny Cater. This turned out to be one of the worst trades in club history. After trading George Scott just after the 1971 season, the Red Sox spent all winter looking for a right-handed, power-hitting first baseman to replace him. Failing in that, they settled on Cater, who was right-handed and played first base, but was a 32-year-old singles hitter, four years older than Scott. It didn't take long for the Red Sox to realize that trading Scott and Lyle was a colossal blunder that cost them the 1972 pennant. Cater began the season as Boston's starting first baseman but lost his job and hit only .237. Lyle, on the other hand, had a 9-5 record for the Yankees, saved 35 games and posted a 1.92 ERA. He finished third in the MVP voting, pitched in three World Series and was named to three All-Star teams. From 1972 through 1977, Lyle had a record of 48-37 with 132 saves and a 2.23 ERA. In 1977, Lyle won the Cy Young Award in a year in which the Sox finished 2½ games behind the Yanks in the AL East. While he was starring in New York, the Red Sox went through an assortment of mediocre closers.

# 23
## March

**O**n this date in 2005, the Red Sox announced that they would stay at Fenway Park for the foreseeable future. Since 1999, the club had been petitioning the city, county and state legislators for a new Fenway to be built just south of the old one. The decision came without conditions, though the club stated it would like to see improvements made to the surrounding neighborhood. "This is a no-strings-attached commitment," said team president Larry Lucchino. Since buying the Red Sox in February 2002, the team's owners made several upgrades and seat additions at Fenway. Those continued after 2005. During the 2005–06 off-season, the .406 Club was rebuilt and became the EMC Club. More luxury boxes were built as well, and additional seating was added to the second level.

# 24
## March

**T**he question of the day. Who are the only two players in baseball history to hit 500 home runs before their 34th birthdays?

Alex Rodriguez hit career-home-run number 500 eight days after his 32nd birthday on August 8, 2007. The first to hit 500 before turning 34 was Jimmie Foxx at 32 years, 336 days. He hit his 500th while playing for the Red Sox on September 24, 1940, during a 16-8 win over the Athletics in Philadelphia. The next youngest after Foxx to reach the 500-home run plateau are Willie Mays (34 years 116 days), Sammy Sosa (34 years, 143 days), Hank Aaron (34 years, 160 days), Babe Ruth (34 years, 186 days) and Ken Griffey, Jr. (34 years, 212 days). At the time he hit number 500, Foxx had the second-most home runs in baseball history, trailing only Ruth's 714. In 1940, Foxx expressed confidence that he could break Ruth's record. According to a system developed by Bill James to predict the likelihood of players reaching career goals, Foxx had a 40 percent chance at the end of the 1940 season of breaking Ruth's record. Foxx never came close to the mark, however. Largely due to injuries, he slowed considerably after 1940 and finished his career in 1945 with 535 home runs. Once second on the all-time home runs list, Foxx had slipped to 16th by 2008.

# 25
## March

**R**ed Sox rookie pitcher Bobby Sprowl was shot in the right arm on this date in 1978 while he and his wife were asleep in the their Winter Haven, Florida, apartment. Sprowl's arm was grazed by a .22-caliber bullet; he was treated at a Winter Haven hospital. The bullet was fired through the wall of an adjacent apartment by a person who though he heard a prowler.

# 26
## March

**T**he question of the day.
　　When did the Red Sox begin
　　wearing uniform numbers?
　　Today, uniform numbers are an
essential part of baseball and play an
important role in a player's identity. It
wasn't until 1931, however, 30 years after the birth of the franchise, that the Sox
began wearing numbers on a permanent
basis. The first numbers that season were issued
to Bill Sweeney (1), Bobby Reeves (2), Jack Rothrock (3), Rabbit
Warstler (4), Otto Miller (5), Hal Rhyne (6), Ollie Marquardt (7),
Pat Creeden (8), Charlie Berry (9), Muddy Ruel (10), Ed Connolly
(11), Russ Scarritt (12), Tom Oliver (14), Earl Webb (15), Johnny
Lucas (16), Al Van Camp (17), Tom Winsett (18), Howie Storie
(19), Milt Gaston (20), Danny MacFayden (21), Jack Russell (22), Ed
Morris (23), Hod Lisenbee (24), Ed Durham (25), Jim Brillheart (27),
Bob Kline (28), Walter Murphy (29), Franklin Milliken (30), Wilcy
Moore (31), manager Shano Collins (32), coach Rudy Hulswitt (33)
and Urbane Pickering (34). No one was originally issued number
13. Those over the years who have braved the superstition while
playing for the Red Sox include Eldon Auker (1939), Reid Nichols
(1985), Billy Joe Robidoux (1990), John Valentin (1992–2001), Rey
Sanchez (2002), Lou Merloni (2003), Doug Mientkiewciz (2004),
Roberto Petagine (2005) and Alex Cora (2006–2008).

# 27
## March

**T**he question of the day.
Which numbers have been retired by the Red Sox?

The first numbers officially retired by the Red Sox were the number 9 of Ted Williams and the number 4 of Joe Cronin, both in 1984. The Sox later retired number 1 for Bobby Doerr in 1988, number 8 for Carl Yastrzemski in 1989, and number 27 for Carlton Fisk in 2000. In addition, Jackie Robinson's number 42 was retired throughout baseball in 1997. For a player to have a number retired by the Red Sox, he must be elected to baseball's Hall of Fame and play 10 years with the club. The retired numbers are displayed on the right-field roof at Fenway Park. From 1989 through 1997, they were arranged in the order they were retired (9-4-1-8) until someone pointed out that 9-4-18 was the day prior to the first game of the 1918 World Series—the last time the club won the Fall Classic. Between the 1997 and 1998 seasons, the Sox sequenced them numerically. Six other Red Sox numbers are in "suspended animation" and weren't issued to anyone in 2008. They are number 5 (Nomar Garciaparra), 6 (Johnny Pesky), 14 (Jim Rice), 21 (Roger Clemens), 26 (Wade Boggs) and 45 (Pedro Martinez).

**B**

# 28
## March

On this date in 1907, Red Sox manager Chick Stahl committed suicide by swallowing three ounces of carbolic acid at the club's spring-training headquarters in West Baden, Indiana. Before dying, Stahl spoke briefly, leaving only the cryptic message: "Boys, I could not help it. It drove me to it." What "it" was perplexed those close to him, as well baseball historians, for over a century. Stahl was born in 1873 and reached the majors as a center fielder with the Boston Braves in 1897. When the Red Sox were formed in 1901, Stahl was one of those who signed with the new club. He was named player-manager in August 1906, succeeding Jimmy Collins, who was also his best friend, and remained with the Sox as the starting third baseman. Under Stahl, the Sox posted a 14-26 record in 1906. He married Julia Harmon of Boston in November 1906, but it was not a happy union. Stahl had been carrying on a liaison with another woman, who had once threatened to shoot him, and impregnated a third during a casual affair. The mistress blackmailed Stahl, threatening to make the affair public, which would have created a major scandal, given the mores of the early 20th century.

# 29
## March

On this date in 2008, the Red Sox defeated the Dodgers 7-4 before 115,300 in an exhibition game at Memorial Coliseum in Los Angeles. It was part of the celebration of the Dodgers' 50th anniversary in L.A. and was the first time the Dodgers played at the facility since 1961. The crowd was the largest in major league history, surpassing the 93,103 for Roy Campanella Night at Memorial Coliseum on May 7, 1959. The Dodgers originally placed 90,000 seats on sale at prices ranging from $10 to $25, with the proceeds going to cancer research. The game sold out in a few hours, prompting the club to put 25,000 standing-room seats on sale. When the Dodgers played at the Coliseum from 1958 through 1961, the left-field foul line was only 251 feet long, topped by a 40-foot-high fence. After 1961, rows of seats 50 feet deep were added at field level. As a result, the configuration for the 2008 exhibition game was even stranger, with a 201-foot foul line and a 60-foot fence. The Dodgers played the game with a two-man outfield and a five-man infield. Kevin Youkilis was the only player to clear the left-field fence with a home run.

B

**30**
**March**

**T**he question of the day. How did Tom Yawkey rebuild Fenway Park during the 1933–34 off-season?

By the time Tom Yawkey bought the Red Sox in February 1933, Fenway Park had deteriorated into a fire trap after nearly 20 years of neglect during the Harry Frazee and Bob Quinn regimes. It was nearly a total reconstruction. Yawkey tore down all of the old wooden stands and replaced them with ones built of steel and concrete, leaving little more than the original steel supports in the grandstand. The foundations and steel supports were also reinforced to provide for a second deck should one be added at a later date. Right and center fields received new steel-and-concrete bleachers. The seating capacity was increased from 27,642 to 37,500. Crews leveled the ten-foot incline in left field and erected a 37-foot-high wall in place of the 25-foot-high wooden fence. The lower 18 feet of the new wall were made of concrete and topped by a 19-foot frame made of railroad ties. Tin covered the concrete and wood. The wall's reinforced steel-and-concrete foundation extended 22 feet below field level. A new scoreboard appeared on the wall. Although remarkably quaint today, it was the first electronically operated scoreboard in baseball with its red, green and yellow lights to indicate balls, strikes and outs.

# 31
## March

**T**he question of the day.
How did a fire affect the
1933–34 rebuilding of Fenway
Park?

While Fenway Park was being
reconstructed, a fire broke out on January 5, 1934, and destroyed part of the
ballpark. The fire lasted five hours and
razed the stands along the left-field foul line
beyond third base, the left-field wall, and the
center-field bleachers. Two workmen were injured. The fire began
when an overturned cement heater ignited tarred canvas used in
the remodeling. Seven hundred workmen fled into the outfield
as the flames spread rapidly, setting fire to the buildings of two
tire companies, three garages and a furniture warehouse behind
the left-field fence. Firemen concentrated most of their efforts on
the oil tanks of the Neponset Oil Company, which was encircled
by flames. The fire turned Tom Yawkey's rebuilding plans into
re-rebuilding plans, but with work crews pulling double shifts, the
ballpark was ready by Opening Day.

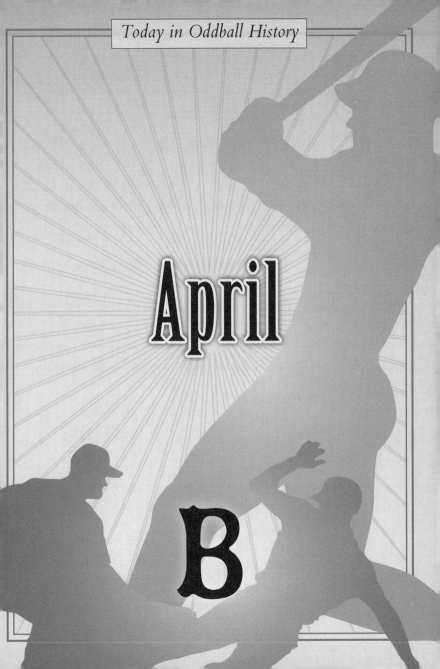

# April

# B

# 01
## April

On this date in 1939, Ted Williams threw a ball out of Ponce de Leon Park in Atlanta after missing a short fly in the eighth inning of an exhibition game against the minor league Atlanta Crackers of the Southern Association. The throw broke a fourth-story window of a building across the street, and manager Joe Cronin took Williams out of the game after the incident. The Red Sox lost the contest 10-9.

# 02
## April

**O**n this date in 1933, the Red Sox narrowly escaped disaster when the club was involved in a train wreck in Wyoming, Delaware, that killed the train's engineer and fireman. The Sox were on the way from Norfolk, Virginia, where the club played an exhibition game, to New York City. A few players were badly shaken, but no one on the Red Sox was seriously injured. Eight of the 12 cars crashed through an open switch while the train was traveling northbound on a southbound track to pass a slow-moving freight train. Seven passengers were hospitalized.

# 03
## April

**T**he question of the day.
When did the Red Sox score 10 runs in the first inning before a batter was retired?

The Red Sox clobbered the Marlins in a record-setting 25-8 win at Fenway Park on June 27, 2003. The Sox set a major league record by scoring 10 runs in the first inning before a batter was retired, tied an American League record for most runs in the first inning of a game with 14 and tied a single-game club record with 28 hits. Johnny Damon tied a major league record for most hits in an inning with three, on a triple, a double and a single. Since 1883, the only other player in the majors to collect three hits in an inning has been Gene Stephens of the Red Sox on June 18, 1953. The half-inning took 50 minutes and 91 pitches to complete and included seven singles, four doubles, a triple, a homer and four walks. The 25 runs represented the second-most in Red Sox history, trailing only the 29-4 win over the Browns in 1950. The game also included a frightening injury and a near brawl. In the seventh inning, Todd Walker's line drive hit Marlins pitcher Kevin Olsen behind the right ear. Olsen was on the ground for nine minutes before being taken off on a stretcher. He didn't pitch in a major league game for the rest of the season.

**B**

**04**
**April**

**H**appy Birthday Gary Geiger. An outfielder with the Red Sox from 1959 through 1965, Gary Geiger was born on this date in 1937. His base-running blunder cost the Sox a victory on June 8, 1961. at Fenway Park. With the score 4-3 in favor of the Angels in the bottom of the 11th, Geiger drove in Chuck Schilling with a triple to tie the score. Unfortunately, Geiger thought the drive won the game, and trotted jubilantly off third. Before he realized his mistake, Geiger was tagged out. Carl Yastrzemski followed with a fly ball that would have scored the winning run with a sacrifice fly if Geiger had remained on third. The game ended in a 4-4 tie at the end of the 11th when a thunderstorm stopped play. Geiger also suffered some unusual ailments during his career. In 1960, he was hospitalized following a collapsed lung in July and missed the remaining two months of the season. Geiger played in only 29 games in 1964 and 1965, following an operation for bleeding ulcers. His big-league career ended in 1970.

# 05
## April

**F**red Snodgrass, a New York Giants outfielder whose muff of a fly ball helped the Red Sox win the 1912 World Series, died on this date in 1974. After seven games, the Series was deadlocked with each team holding three victories. Game two resulted in a tie. The Giants took a 2-1 lead in the top of the 10th in the deciding eighth game at Fenway Park, played on October 16. Snodgrass missed an easy fly ball to centerfield, which lead to the Giants' loss of the game and the Series. Snodgrass's dropped fly ball became known as the "$30,000 muff," which was the difference between the winner's and loser's share. It haunted him to his grave. When Snodgrass died, more than 61 years after the event, his obituary in the *New York Times* was headlined: "Fred Snodgrass, 86, Dead, Ballplayer Muffed 1912 Fly."

**06**
**April**

On this date in 1939, the exhibition game between the Red Sox and Reds in Florence, South Carolina, was called with the score 18-18 in the ninth inning because the clubs ran out of baseballs. The farcical contest, which seemed to have been scripted by the Marx Brothers, was played in a 50-mile-per-hour gale on a field with no grass in the infield, causing a game-long dust storm. So many balls were blown into the crowd and out of the ballpark that the game ended because the supply of 54 baseballs was completely exhausted. Most of the players ended the game capless with their uniforms covered with dust. Many played in jackets to protect themselves from the inclement conditions. The starting pitcher for the Red Sox was, appropriately, Denny Galehouse. Five days later, the Sox lost 11-9 to the Reds in an exhibition game played on historic ground in Petersburg, Virginia. The ball field was located on the Civil War battlefield where General Robert E. Lee and the Confederate Army made their last stand in 1865 before surrendering at Appomattox. On April 12, the Red Sox and Reds continued their unusual trip north by playing on a diamond laid out on the football field in Roanoke, Virginia, with the center-field fence only 260 feet from home plate. The Sox won by the football-like score of 17-14.

# 07
## April

**T**he question of the day.
When did the Red Sox hit into two triple plays in one game? The Red Sox became the only major league team in history to hit into two triple plays in one game on July 17, 1990, but overcame the miscues to win 1-0 over the Twins at Fenway Park. It is also the only contest in major league history in which two triple plays have been recorded. Both were started by third baseman Gary Gaetti, who fielded a bases-loaded smash by Tom Brunansky in the fourth inning and Jody Reed's sharp grounder in the eighth with runners on first and second. On both plays, Gaetti stepped on third and threw to second baseman Al Newman, who relayed to Kent Hrbek at first. The Boston base runners retired were Reed and Carlos Quintana in the fourth and Tim Naehring and Wade Boggs in the eighth. The very next day, the Red Sox hit into six double plays, including five in the first five innings, and won again 6-4 over Minnesota in Boston. The Sox helped themselves with four double plays of their own. A day after setting a record for the most triple plays in a game (two) the two clubs combined to set a another mark for the most double plays in a contest (10).

**08 April**

On this date in 1916, the Red Sox traded center fielder Tris Speaker to the Indians for Sad Sam Jones, Fred Thomas and $55,000. Speaker was one of the top players in the game at the time of the trade. He was 28 years old and had a career batting average of .337 and an on-base percentage of .414 in 1,065 games. The deal was completed during contentious salary negotiations between Speaker and the Red Sox. The Sox wanted to slash Speaker's paycheck in half from $18,000 to $9,000, and he refused to sign his contract. Although the Red Sox would win the World Series in 1916 and 1918 without Speaker, the club definitely came out on the short end of the deal. An angry Speaker hit .386 in 1916 to win the American League batting title. It was the only time between 1907 and 1919 that Ty Cobb failed to lead the league in batting average. Speaker retained his superstar level of play well into the 1920s. It took Jones until 1918 to win his first game for the Red Sox, although he had a couple of effective seasons in Boston. Thomas contributed nothing to the Red Sox' fortunes. Among Red Sox players, Speaker still ranks third in batting average, fourth in on-base percentage, second in stolen bases (267) and second in triples (106)

# 09
## April

**T**he question of the day.
How did a sportswriter change the distance markers at Fenway Park?

From 1934 through 1995, the distance from home plate to the left-field wall was listed at 315 feet. Many believed it was shorter than that, but the Red Sox wouldn't allow anyone to measure it. During the first home stand in 1995, *Boston Globe* columnist Dan Shaughnessy measured the distance with a 100-foot Stanley Steelmaster Long Tape. The distance, according to Shaughnessy's calculations, was 309 feet, three inches. In mid-May of that year, after Shaughnessy's story appeared in the *Globe*, the Sox put up a new sign reading 310 feet. "That's about what it is," admitted groundskeeper Joe Mooney. "We rounded it off. It

**10**
**April**

**T**railing 7-2 in the home opener on this date in 1998, the Red Sox staged an incredible seven-run rally in the ninth inning, capped by Mo Vaughn's walk-off grand slam, to defeat the Mariners 9-7. Through eight innings, Randy Johnson allowed only two hits and struck out 15 batters, but he was removed after throwing 131 pitches. The Sox scored their seven runs off four relievers without a batter being retired. Troy O'Leary led off with a single and Mark Lemke walked before Darren Bragg drove in the first run with a double. Mike Benjamin walked to load the bases and Nomar Garciaparra drove in the second tally with a single. John Valentin was hit by a pitch to force in a run and make the score 7-5. Vaughn ended the game with his slam off Paul Spoljaric. In addition, there was no beer sold at the ballpark for the first time since Prohibition in 1933 because the opener fell on Good Friday.

**B**

# 11
## April

**F**ive days after the United States declared war on Germany and entered World War I, the Red Sox defeated the Yankees 10-3 on Opening Day at the Polo Grounds in New York on this date in 1917. Dick Hoblitzel homered for the Red Sox. Tilly Walker contributed two triples and a double. It had snowed six inches in New York City the previous two days, and the snow had to be cleared from the diamond. Major General Leonard Wood threw out the ceremonial first pitch and reviewed a military drill conducted by the Yankee players. As a show of patriotism during the war, major leaguers often performed military drills prior to games in 1917 with bats on their shoulders simulating weapons. American League president Ban Johnson offered a $500 prize to the team with the best drills, which were judged by military experts. The Browns won, with the Red Sox finishing fifth among the eight teams in the league.

# 12
## April

**O**n this date in 1992, Red Sox pitcher Matt Young pitched an eight-inning complete game without allowing a hit, but lost 2-1 to the Indians in the first game of a double-header in Cleveland. The Indians scored a run in the first inning when Kenny Lofton walked, stole second and third, and scored on an error by shortstop Luis Rivera. In the third, Cleveland added its second run on two walks, a force play and a fielder's choice. Young walked seven and struck out five. He doesn't get credit for a no-hitter in the official record books, however, because he failed to pitch nine innings. As the home team with a lead, the Indians didn't bat in the ninth. Cleveland won without a hit a day after collecting 20 hits and losing 7-5 in a 19-inning game against the Sox. In the second game of the April 12 double-header, Roger Clemens added another terrific performance with a two-hitter to defeat the Indians 3-0. Clemons wasn't scheduled to start: he'd been left behind in Boston to prepare for a start against the Orioles at Fenway Park on April 13. But the 19-inning game on April 11 depleted the pitching staff, so Clemens volunteered to fly to Cleveland for the April 12 contest. Young had little success after his truncated no-hitter.

# 13
## April

**T**he question of the day.

How did Ted Williams change the field dimensions at Fenway Park?

During Williams's rookie year in 1939, it was 332 feet from home plate to the right-field foul pole and 402 feet to the right-field power alley. He hit 31 homers that season, with 14 struck at Fenway. Between the 1939 and 1940 seasons, the right-field dimensions were shortened. The most significant modification was the construction of the bullpens in front of the bleachers. This reduced the home-run distance in the power alley to 382 feet. The seating area down the right-field line also changed. In 1934, the Red Sox constructed a pavilion along the right-field line with 8,900 uncomfortable bench seats that were unpopular with fans. It went largely unoccupied except on days the grandstand and bleachers were full. The team tore down the pavilion between the 1939 and 1940 seasons and replaced it with an extension of the grandstand containing individual seats. The new grandstand configuration wrapped around the right-field corner and reduced the distance down the line from 332 feet to 302, another move to help Williams with long drives. During his career, Williams hit 248 home runs at Fenway and 273 on the road.

**B**

# 14
## April

In one of the most sensational debuts in major league history, 21-year-old Red Sox pitcher Billy Rohr came within one strike of a no-hitter on this date in 1967 for a 3-0 victory over Whitey Ford and the Yankees in the first game of the season at Yankee Stadium. With none out in the ninth, Carl Yastrzemski made a spectacular catch in left to snag a drive over his head struck by Tom Tresh. Yaz landed on his knee and did a complete somersault. Joe Pepitone lifted a lazy fly to right fielder Tony Conigliaro for the second out. Rohr took Elston Howard to a 3-2 count, only to have Howard line a single into right-center for the Yankees' only hit. The normally partisan New York crowd booed Howard before Rohr retired Charley Smith for the final out. Rohr walked five batters and struck out two. In his second start, on April 21, Rohr beat the Yankees 6-1 with the lone run coming on an eighth-inning home run by Howard. Rohr never won another game for the Sox, however, and was back in the minors in June. He pitched 17 games for the Indians in 1968, but won only one game. In his first two big-league starts, Rohr was 2-0 with an ERA of 0.50. Over the rest of his career, he had a record of 1-3 and an earned run average of 7.80.

**B**

# 15
## April

**T**he question of the day.
Who holds the Red Sox record for most total bases in a game?

In a devastating display of power, Fred Lynn collected 16 total bases and drove in 10 runs with three homers, a triple and a single during a 15-1 romp over the Tigers in Detroit on June 18, 1975. Lynn had seven RBIs after only three innings. He hit a two-run homer off Joe Coleman in the first inning, a three-run homer against Coleman in the second and a two-run triple facing Lerrin LaGrow in the third that hit the outfield fence about three feet from the top. After beating out a single in the eighth, Lynn capped the evening with a three-run homer off Tom Walker in the ninth. The 16 total bases also tied an American league record. By season's end, Lynn was not only the American League Rookie of the Year, but the MVP as well. He hit .331 with 21 homers and 105 RBIs in 1975, led the league in runs (103) and doubles (47) and drew favorable comparisons to Stan Musial, all at the age of 23. With the exception of 1979, however, Lynn never reached those numbers again in a career that ended after 1,969 games in 1990 with a .283 batting average and 306 home runs.

**B**

**16 April**

**H**appy Birthday Jim Lonborg. Born on this date in 1942, Jim Lonborg will be forever remembered for his 22-9 record and pennant-clinching victory on the final game of the 1967 season. The previous day, the Red Sox moved into a first-place tie by beating the Twins 6-4. Heading into the final contest, the Red Sox and Twins both had records of 91-70, and the Tigers were 90-70. Lonborg started against Minnesota's Dean Chance. Lonborg had a 0-6 career record against the Twins. In the sixth inning, the Sox exploded for five runs to take a 5-2 lead. The Twins scored in the eighth in a rally cut short by a brilliant catch by Carl Yastrzemski. It was 5-3 heading into the ninth. Lonborg retired the Twins on an infield single, a double play and a pop-up by Russ Nixon to Rico Petrocelli at short. Fans swarmed onto the field and lifted Lonborg like a tidal wave. He was carried all the way into right field before being rescued by policemen, but not before fans pulled off his shirt, took his hat and even stole his shoelaces. The pennant race wasn't completely over, however, when the game ended. The Tigers still had a chance to tie for the lead in the race and force a one-game playoff against the Sox by sweeping the Angels in a double-header. The Tigers won the opener fvcc 6-4, but lost the nightcap 8-5, giving the Sox the pennant dubbed the "Impossible Dream."

# 17
## April

**O**n this date in 1904, General Charles H. Taylor, publisher of the *Boston Globe*, purchased the Red Sox from Henry Killilea. Taylor outbid John Fitzgerald, Boston mayor and grandfather of future President John Kennedy, to buy the Sox. Taylor bought the club for his son John I. Taylor, a bon vivant around town who showed no interest in his father's newspaper operation. John loved sports, and his father figured running the Red Sox would keep him busy and out of trouble. Taylor's ownership of the Sox was often marked by reckless, erratic and impetuous decisions. He took the 1904 pennant-winners to last place in 1906, then rebuilt the club into world champions by 1912. Taylor's legacy still lives in two important ways. In 1907, he selected Red Sox as the team nickname. In 1911, he chose the site of a new ballpark on a five-sided block surrounded by Lansdowne, Ipswich, Van Ness and Jersey Streets and Brookline Avenue. A year later the ballpark opened as Fenway Park.

**B**

**18**
**April**

**O**n this date in 1950, the Red Sox blew a nine-run lead to the Yankees at Fenway Park and lost 15-10 before an Opening Day crowd of 31,822. The match-up had been anticipated for months after the Yankees won the final two games of the 1949 season to steal the AL pennant from the Sox. The Sox led 9-0 after five innings with Mel Parnell on the mound. The *Boston American* hit the streets with the headline "Sox Romp." But the Yankees broke loose with four runs in the sixth. The Red Sox scored again in the seventh to pull ahead 10-4 before the Yankees exploded for eight runs in the eighth off five pitchers, then added three more in the ninth. In his major league debut, Billy Martin had two hits in the eight-run eighth. Billy Goodman homered for the Red Sox. It was only his second major league homer and the first since 1948.

# 19
## April

**O**n this date in 1902, the Red Sox opened the season at Huntington Grounds on Patriots' Day and rallied for four runs in the ninth inning to stun the Orioles 7-6. To take advantage of the holiday, which fell on a Saturday in 1902, the Red Sox and Orioles opened the season four days ahead of the rest of the American League.

The entrances to the ballpark proved to be insufficient to handle the unexpectedly large crowd, and the fences collapsed before the wild, surging mob. Several thousands entered the grounds for free, leaving attendance at the game open for speculation. Estimates varied wildly.

**B**

**20**
**April**

**W**ith 27,000 attending, the Red Sox played their first regular-season game at Fenway Park on this date in 1920 and defeated the Yankees 7-6 in 11 innings. The loser hurler was Hippo Vaughn. There were concerns early in the season about the small crowds at Fenway. "The fact that the park is not as handy to reach and get away from [as Huntington Grounds] has hurt some," wrote Tim Murnane in *The Sporting News,* "and will until people get accustomed to the new direction." Fans complained that the less-expensive bleacher section was farther away from the action at Fenway compared to the old ballpark. "On account of the size of the park, and the entrances being on two widely separated ends of the grounds, I find much of the sociability gone," added Murnane. Despite the leap from fifth place in 1911 to first in 1912, along with the attraction of the new park, attendance increased only 18 percent, from 503,961 to 597,096.

# 21
## April

**B**illy Sullivan, former publicity director of the Boston Braves, announced plans on this date in 1958 to build a 65,000-seat stadium in Norwood, Massachusetts, 14 miles north of Boston. Sullivan hoped that the stadium would house the Red Sox and attract a pro football team to the Boston area. Sullivan was the head of a local oil company. Sullivan never got his Norwood stadium built, but in November 1959, became one of the founding members of the American Football League as the owner of the Boston Patriots. One of Sullivan's original partners was ex-Red Sox star Dom DiMaggio. The AFL began play in 1960. The Patriots played at Boston University's Nickerson Field (the site of old Braves Field) from 1960 through 1962, Fenway Park from 1963 through 1968, Boston College's Alumni Field in 1969 and Harvard Stadium in 1970. Sullivan finally built a stadium of his own in 1971 with the opening of Foxborough's Schaefer Stadium, which was later known as Sullivan Stadium. In conjunction with the move to Foxborough, the Boston Patriots were renamed the New England Patriots.

**B**

**22**
**April**

**D**uring a nationally televised contest on ESPN on this date in 2007, the Red Sox clobbered four home runs in a row off Chase Wright and beat the Yankees 7-6 at Fenway Park. Holding a 3-0 lead, Wright retired the first two batters in the third inning. Manny Ramirez hit the first home run deep into the Green Monster seats. On a 1-2 pitch, J. D. Drew homered into the center-field seats above the bullpen. Mike Lowell smashed a 1-1 pitch over the Green Monster. Jason Varitek did the same to a 1-0 offering. Wright became only the second pitcher in baseball history to allow four consecutive homers. The first was Paul Foytack of the 1963 Angels. The Yankees rallied from Wright's debacle to take a 5-4 lead into seventh. Lowell put the Sox into the lead for good with a three-run homer.

# 23
## April

**T**ed Williams hit his first career homer on this date in 1939 with a first-inning blast against Bud Thomas during a 12-8 loss to the Athletics at Fenway Park. The ball went 420 feet and landed in the right-center-field bleachers. Williams also had a double and two singles. He missed a fifth hit when A's left fielder Bob Johnson caught a liner against the wall. Williams finished his career with 521 home runs. Other famous first homers struck by players in a Red Sox uniform include those of Babe Ruth and Carl Yastrzemski. The first of Ruth's 714 was hit off Jack Warhop of the Yankees on May 6, 1915, during a 13-inning, 4-3 Red Sox loss at the Polo Grounds in New York. Yaz hit 452 career homers. The first was on May 9, 1961, off Jerry Casale during an 8-7 loss to the Angels in Los Angeles at Dodger Stadium.

# 24
## April

**T**he question of the day.
How did Tom Yawkey plan to enlarge Fenway Park in 1958?
During the 1958 season, Tom Yawkey requested that the city close Lansdowne Street behind the left-field wall, tear down the wall and the businesses on the other side of the street, extend the left-field line to 330 feet and build additional stands. With the construction of the Massachusetts Turnpike just north of Fenway, Yawkey desired a special road directly from the turnpike to the ballpark. The baseball club also wanted to pave some nearby parkland to create parking space for 4,000 cars. The city of Boston and the state of Massachusetts failed to approve the changes, however, and the Green Monster remained in place.

# 25
## April

**T**he question of the day. How did Tom Yawkey plan to replace Fenway Park during the 1960s?

Patriots owner Billy Sullivan chaired a stadium commission in 1963 that drew interest from the Red Sox. He wanted to build a multi-purpose stadium with a retractable roof, hotel and garage in the South Station area. Tom Yawkey believed that Fenway Park was too small, too old, too expensive to maintain, too difficult to reach by car and had insufficient parking. Yawkey wanted the Sox to play in a stadium similar to those built in Atlanta, Cincinnati, St. Louis, Pittsburgh and Philadelphia, with a capacity of 50,000–60,000 and artificial turf. He also wanted the government to foot the bill for the new stadium project. City, county and state officials had other priorities, however, and the stadium project became mired in Boston and Massachusetts politics. Citing financial losses, Yawkey warned in June 1967 that the Red Sox and Patriots might both leave Boston if a stadium wasn't built. He added that in five years, he doubted that the club would still be playing at Fenway. The stadium proposal had the backing of Governor John Volpe, and funding was approved in the Massachusetts House of Representatives, but in July 1968, the Massachusetts Senate killed two stadium bills, which saved Fenway Park from the wrecking ball.

# 26
## April

**T**he Red Sox played the first game in franchise history on this date in 1901 and lost 10-6 to the Orioles in Baltimore. The starting, and losing, pitcher was Win Kellum. The lineup for the game consisted of Tommy Dowd (lf), Charlie Hemphill (rf), Chick Stahl (cf), Jimmy Collins (3b), Buck Freeman (1b), Freddie Parent (ss), Hobe Ferris (2b), Lou Criger (c) and Kellum (p). Prior to the game, a noontime parade of 40 carriages containing officials and players from both clubs, along with representatives of the trade unions, manufacturing concerns, and sporting organizations was held, starting at the Eutaw House Hotel (near today's Camden Yards) and ending at Oriole Park. The Red Sox and Orioles were cheered by thousands along the route, and homes and businesses were decorated for the occasion. At the ballpark, Red Sox players were presented with a floral scroll bearing the inscription, "Welcome Boston." A native of Canada, Kellum quickly became a footnote in Red Sox history. He pitched only six games with the club, compiling a 2-3 record and a 6.38 ERA. During the game, Larry McLean, also a Canadian, became the first pinch-hitter in AL history and collected a double.

# 27
## April

**O**n this date in 2002, Derek Lowe pitched a no-hitter to defeat the Devil Rays 10-0 at Fenway Park. It was the first no-hitter in Boston since 1965. The only base runner was Brent Abernathy, who walked leading off the third inning. In the ninth, Lowe retired Russ Johnson on a soft liner to second baseman Rey Sanchez, Felix Escalona on a fly ball to Rickey Henderson in center field, and Jason Tyner on a grounder to Sanchez. Lowe's catcher was Jason Varitek. The two came to Boston together in a trade with the Mariners in 1997. Lowe struck out six and threw 96 pitches. Heading into the 2002 season, he was 28 years old and had appeared in 298 big-league games, but only 22 as a starter. During the 2000 and 2001 campaigns, Lowe saved 66 games as the Sox closer. In a bold experiment, he was converted into a full-time starter in 2002. Lowe responded with a 21-8 record and a 2.58 ERA.

# 28
### April

**T**he question of the day.
When did the Red Sox and Athletics combine for 26 doubles in a double-header?

The Sox and A's brought new meaning to the phrase double-header by combining for 26 two-baggers on July 8, 1905 in Philadelphia. Most of them were of the ground-rule variety hit into the overflow crowd of 25,000. The first game was delayed for half an hour to get the crowd under control. Ropes were stretched across the outfield, but the crowd was 20 feet deep behind the outfielders. Others were in foul ground within a few feet of first and third base and 10 to 15 feet from home plate. Many standing in foul territory were injured by foul balls. The Red Sox scored six runs in the fourth inning of the first game, mostly on ground-rule doubles. With the A's at bat in the bottom of the fourth, bleacher fans began throwing cushions at foul-line spectators, and several fights ensued. Police were called in and arrests were made; fans surged onto the field. More police were called in, and by the time they arrived, a few fans were seated on the pitcher's mound. After a 30-minute delay, the crowd was driven back so the game could continue. The Red Sox won the first game 11-8, but lost the second, called after eight innings by darkness, 11-4.

# 29
## April

**O**n this date in 1986, Roger Clemens broke a major league record with 20 strikeouts during a 3-1 win over the Mariners at Fenway Park. He had 14 strikeouts in the first six innings, including an American League record-tying eight in a row. Clemens tied the previous record for strikeouts in a nine-inning game of 19 shared by Tom Seaver, Nolan Ryan and Steve Carlton by fanning Spike Owen to start the ninth. Clemens then struck out Phil Bradley for the record before inducing Ken Phelps to ground out to end the game. Clemens recorded 20 strikeouts without walking a batter. He allowed three hits, one of them a home run to Gorman Thomas in the seventh, and threw 138 pitches. Clemens was not only the first pitcher to fan 20 in a nine-inning game, but the second as well. He struck out 20 again on September 19, 1996, defeating the Tigers 4-0 in Detroit. Clemons threw 151 pitches, surrendered four hits and didn't walk a batter. He struck out the side in the second, fifth and sixth innings. Clemens entered the ninth with 19 strikeouts, but Alan Trammell popped out, Ruben Sierra singled and Tony Clark flied out. Travis Fryman struck out to end the game.

**B**

**30 April**

**A**fter defeats in the first three games of the 1901 season, the Red Sox achieved the first victory in franchise history on this date by defeating the Athletics 8-6 in Philadelphia. The Athletics jumped ahead 6-1, but the Sox chipped away. Boston tied the game 6-6 on a two-run homer over the right-field fence by Buck Freeman in the ninth inning, the first round-tripper in Red Sox history. The Sox scored two 10th-inning runs on a base on balls and three hits in the American League's first ever extra-inning game. Cy Young was the winning pitcher.

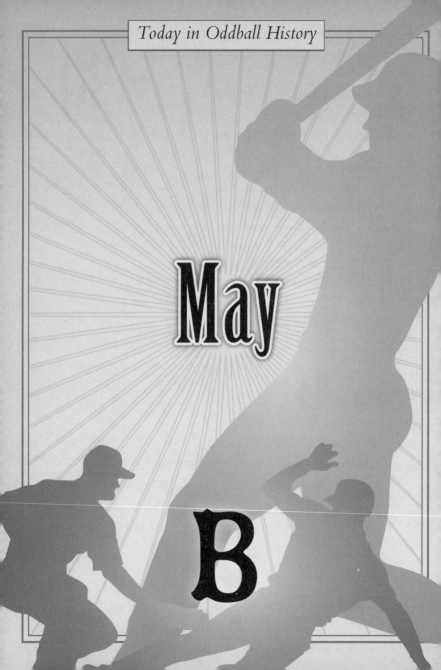

# May

B

**01**
**May**

**O**n this date in 1902, umpire Jack Sheridan barely escaped with his life following a 6-4 Red Sox win over the Orioles in Baltimore. In the ninth inning, Orioles player-manager John McGraw was hit by a pitch from Boston's Bill Dinneen, but Sheridan refused to allow McGraw first base, claiming he stepped into the pitch. McGraw was ejected in the ensuing argument. At the conclusion of the game, the crowd surged onto the field and surrounded Sheridan. A cordon of 12 police officers escorted the umpire to a waiting trolley car. One fan threw a brick, which struck one of the officers on the lip, opening a nasty cut.

# 02
## May

**T**he question of the day. Which Boston native hit a home run in his first at-bat with the Red Sox?

Eddie Pellagrini hit a home run in his first major league plate appearance on April 22, 1946. His homer broke a 4-4 tie in the seventh inning and gave the Red Sox a 5-4 victory over the Senators at Fenway Park. Pellagrini entered the game in the fifth inning at shortstop when Johnny Pesky left after being hit in the head with a pitch. Pellagrini grew up in the Boston neighborhood of Dorchester and was 28 years old when he made his big-league debut. He played two seasons with the Red Sox at the start of a big-league career that ended in 1954 with 20 homers and a .226 batting average while playing for five teams. He was extremely superstitious about the number 13 and wore it on his uniform while playing for the Phillies, Reds and Pirates. Eddie was born on March 13 and married a woman born on the 13th. He went so far as to sign his contract each season on the 13th of the month. Pellagrini finished his career with 13 triples and 13 stolen bases and was hit by pitches 13 times. He was later the baseball coach at Boston College from 1958 through 1988 and guided the team to three College World Series.

**B**

**03**
**May**

**O**n this date in 1994, the Red Sox lost two pitchers to injury in the third inning of a 7-6 win over the Mariners at Fenway Park. Frank Viola left with an injured elbow, which popped when he was pitching to Eric Anthony. Paul Quantrill relieved Viola and threw a high-and-tight pitch to Anthony. After Anthony walked, he went halfway to first, then charged the mound, causing both benches to empty. In the ensuing brawl, Quantrill ended up at the bottom of the pile-up and had to leave the game with an injured finger. Viola had to undergo Tommy John transplant surgery and never pitched another game with the Sox.

# 04
## May

**T**he question of the day. Which catcher was kicked in the posterior by his own manager on the field?

During a 12-2 loss in the first game of a double-header in Cleveland on August 1, 1948, Lou Boudreau of the Indians stole home on a close play at the plate. Red Sox manager Joe McCarthy came out to argue the call, but he was just as angry at catcher Matt Batts for allowing Boudreau to score as he was at the umpire. McCarthy kicked Batts in the rear end, but later denied doing so despite thousands of witnesses. McCarthy's disposition didn't improve when the Sox lost the second tilt 6-1. Batts also refused to fly and took the train whenever the club traveled by air. His fear of flying stemmed from an incident during World War II. Batts was on a transport plane when he opened a window because it was hot. As a practical joke, the pilot went into a dive and the change in air pressure sent Batts to the roof of the plane and nearly sucked him out of the window.

**05**
**May**

**P**itching the first no-hitter in Red Sox history, Cy Young hurled a perfect game on this date in 1904 to defeat the Athletics 3-0 before 10,267 at Huntington Grounds. Young fanned six and allowed only six balls out of the infield. The perfect game by Young was part of a major league-record 24 consecutive hitless innings. On April 25, Young allowed no hits over the last three innings of a 2-0 loss to the Athletics in Philadelphia. On April 30, Young relieved George Winter in the third inning and held the Senators hitless the rest of the way in a 4-1 win at Washington. On May 11, Young pitched a 15-inning complete game to win 1-0 over the Tigers in Boston. He yielded no hits until the sixth inning when Sam Crawford singled to break Young's hitless streak. Young also set a club record with 45 consecutive scoreless innings during the 1904 season.

# 06
## May

**O**n this date in 1918, Babe Ruth played at a position other than pitcher in a regular-season game for the first time, starting at first base and batting sixth during a 10-3 loss to the Yankees at the Polo Grounds in New York. In the fourth inning, the Babe hit a home run into the upper deck in right field. Ruth made his major league debut in 1914. The Red Sox had contemplated moving Ruth to first base or the outfield for several years, but turning one of the best pitchers in the game into a hitter was a risk the club was unwilling to take. Many suggested that Ruth remain in the pitching rotation and play in the field between starts, but there were worries that Ruth would injure his valuable arm, especially on a throw from the outfield. There were many reasons that Ruth was converted from a pitcher to an outfielder, but it was World War I that tipped the balance. Because of military inductions and enlistments, the club's depth on offense was cut dangerously thin. The pitching staff was left relatively unscathed by the service defections. In May of 1918, Ruth was simply the best alternative for the lack of offensive production that the Sox suffered in both the outfield and at first.

**07**
**May**

**H**appy Birthday Dick Williams. The manager of the Red Sox from 1967 through 1969, Dick Williams was born on this date in 1929. In contrast to his predecessors, Williams was a strict taskmaster. His tough, brusque demeanor proved to be just what the lethargic, jaded and self-ish Red Sox needed when he was hired on September 28, 1966. The club hadn't posted a winning season since 1958, were 62-100 in 1965 and finished 1966 with a 72-90 record in ninth place in a ten-team league. In 1967, Williams took the Red Sox to their first World Series since 1946. As a player, he spent 14 seasons in the majors for five different clubs from 1951 through 1964, mostly in a utility role with a reputation as an individual who would give his last drop of blood to win. Williams ended his playing career with the Red Sox in 1963 and 1964. In 1965 and 1966, he managed the Red Sox Class AAA farm club in Toronto in the International League. When he was elevated to the parent club, Williams made it clear that he had assumed total command. With his crew cut and sharp tongue, he had the air of a Marine drill sergeant and used any means necessary to motivate his players, including benchings and public ridicule. It all worked in 1967 with the "Impossible Dream" pennant, but by 1969, Williams was fired when the club was unable to repeat the miracle.

# 08
## May

**O**n this day in 1926, a fire erupted at Fenway Park just after the crowd cleared following a 10-4 loss to the Indians. Before the fire department could arrive, Red Sox manager Lee Fohl and a handful of park employees fought the fire with ground-skeepers' hoses, but it was too late. The grass caught fire and spread to a billboard. The wooden bleachers, which had been the scene of three fires the day before, were destroyed. Flying embers kept the firemen fighting blazes all around the grandstand and properties surrounding Fenway. It took nearly an hour to extinguish the blaze. The fire department said the fire was accidental, but given that it was the fourth fire in the same place in less than 36 hours, the circumstances were suspicious. The bleachers weren't replaced until 1934, leaving a huge cinder-strewn expanse in foul territory along the left-field line. For eight years, the ground beyond the grandstand was the largest foul territory in the major leagues. Foul balls hit past the stands down the left-field line remained in play all the way to the fence paralleling Jersey Street (now Yawkey Way) and Brookline Avenue.

**09**
**May**

**T**he question of the day.
How did a pantomime act by Eddie Kasko get him ejected from a game?

With the Red Sox leading 3-2 in the ninth inning of a game against the Angels in Anaheim on July 7, 1972, Boston's Ben Oglivie was called safe by umpire Hank Morganweck on a close play at the plate while sidestepping catcher Jeff Torborg. The Angels claimed Oglivie was out of the base line. Morganweck huddled with second-base umpire John Rice and reversed his decision, calling Oglivie out. Red Sox manager Eddie Kasko exploded from the dugout. When words failed him, Kasko keeled over backwards on the grass as if he had fainted from disbelief over the call. The umpires weren't amused by Kasko's pantomime act and threw him out. Kasko followed as much of the game as he could from a tunnel beneath the dugout. He blew his stack again over a 10th-inning umpiring decision, ran onto the field and was ejected again. In the end, the Red Sox won 5-3 on Oglivie's two-run homer in the 10th.

# 10
## May

**O**n this date in 1999, Nomar Garciaparra hit three homers, including two grand slams, and racked up 10 RBIs to lead the Red Sox to a 12-4 win over the Mariners at Fenway Park. Garciaparra hit a grand slam off Brett Hinchliffe in the first inning. Nomar then sliced a two-run shot off Hinchliffe in the third that curved around the right-field foul pole. After fouling out in the fourth, and walking in the sixth, Garciaparra hit his second grand slam in the eighth while facing Eric Weaver. The 10 RBIs tied a club record with Rudy York ( July 27, 1946), Norm Zauchin (May 27, 1955) and Fred Lynn ( June 18, 1975). Through 2008, 12 players have hit two grand slams in a game. Garciaparra is the only one of the 12 to accomplish the feat at home. The other 11 were all on the road.

**11**
**May**

**T**he question of the day.
What was the greatest ninth-inning rally in Red Sox history?

The most incredible ninth-inning rally in club history took place in the first game of a double-header on June 18, 1961, when the Red Sox scored eight runs with two out to beat the Senators 13-12 at Fenway Park. Washington scored five in the top half to take what appeared to be an insurmountable 12-5 advantage. In the bottom half, a single by Don Buddin was sandwiched between two outs before nine batters in a row reached base for the win. Singles by Chuck Schilling and Carroll Hardy drove in Buddin. Gary Geiger walked to load the bases and Dave Sisler came in as the new Senators pitcher to replace Carl Mathias. Sisler immediately issued base on balls to Jackie Jensen and Frank Malzone to force in two more runs and narrow the gap to 12-8. With the bases still full, Jim Pagliaroni stepped to the plate and hit a grand slam to tie the game. Vic Wertz got aboard on a walk and Marty Kutyna replaced Sisler. Wertz scored the winning run with the help of two singles by Buddin and Russ Nixon, the latter as a pinch-hitter. Ted Wills was the winning pitcher despite giving up three runs in two-thirds of an inning. In the second game, Pagliaroni clubbed another dramatic homer in the 13th inning to lift the Sox to a 6-5 victory.

**12 May**

**O**n this date in 1953, Dom DiMaggio announced his retirement, effective immediately. DiMaggio was the club's starting center fielder from 1940 through 1952, with the exception of three years (1943–45) when he was in the service. In spring training, he lost his job to Tom Umphlett, and DiMaggio had three at-bats in the first four weeks of the 1953 season. Umphlett was 23 years old and part of the Red Sox' massive youth movement. Other young players on the 1953 roster included Billy Consolo (18), Gene Stephens (20), Dick Brodowski (20), Faye Throneberry (22), Milt Bolling (22), Karl Olson (22), Leo Kiely (23), Norm Zauchin (23), Jimmy Piersall (23), Ike Delock (23), Frank Sullivan (23), Mickey McDermott (24), Dick Gernert (24) and Bill Henry (25). The contingent was named "Boudreau's Babes" after manager Lou Boudreau. More youthful talent arrived in 1954 and 1955 with the likes of Frank Malzone, Tom Brewer, Harry Agganis, Russ Kemmerer, Tex Clevenger, Pete Daley and Frank Baumann. Many experts predicted that this group would form a dynasty in Boston, but none of them came close to playing on a pennant-winner with the Red Sox.

**13 May**

On this date in 1955, Ted Williams ended his retirement by signing a contract. In what he said would be the final game of his career, Williams hit a home run during an 11-2 win over the Senators at Fenway Park on September 26, 1954. Few believed he was serious about retiring, and the Red Sox kept him on the active roster, even after he held out in spring training and the first month of the regular season. Williams and his wife, Doris, filed for divorce in December 1954, and the divorce became final in a Miami court on May 9. Two days later, he reached a financial settlement with her. The ink was barely dry on the settlement when Williams "unretired" and returned to the Red Sox. The timing of his retirement and eventual return strongly suggests that the "retirement" was designed to exclude the new contract from the divorce settlement. Williams played his first game in 1955 on May 28 and finished the season with a .356 batting average and 28 homers in 98 games. He didn't retire permanently until 1960.

**B**

# 14
## May

**T**he question of the day. Who was Carroll Hardy? Carroll Hardy played only 433 games as an outfielder with four clubs, including the Red Sox, from 1958 through 1967, but had a fascinating career. Before embarking on a baseball career, Hardy played halfback for the San Francisco 49ers in 1955, scoring four touchdowns. While playing for the Indians in 1958, Hardy hit his first big-league homer on his 25th birthday as a pinch-hitter for Roger Maris. He was acquired by the Red Sox in 1960, and on September 20 became the only player ever to pinch-hit for Ted Williams when Ted was forced to leave the game after fouling a pitch off his ankle. In 1961, Hardy pinch-hit for Carl Yastrzemski. On August 25 of that year, he hit a grand slam the day before his wife gave birth to a daughter. On April 11, 1962, Hardy hit a walk-off grand slam in the 12th inning to account for all four runs of a 4-0 win over the Indians at Fenway Park. The homer was struck off Ron Taylor, who started the contest and was making his major league debut. The four runs were the only ones the Red Sox scored in the first three games of the 1962 season. Hardy was traded to Houston for Dick Williams in 1962. In the 1970s, Hardy was the player-personnel director of the Denver Broncos and helped put together the famed "Orange Crush" defense.

**15
May**

**O**n this date in 1999, the Red Sox announced plans for a 44,000-seat stadium to be built some 600 feet south of Fenway Park. The team hoped to play in the new park in 2003. The $550 million plan included $350 million for stadium construction. The new ballpark would have all the desired modern amenities, such as luxury boxes, preferred seating and expanded concessions. In an attempt to appease preservationists, plans called for retaining much of the famed Green Monster in a park area and part of the original tapestry wall along Yawkey Way as part of a grand entranceway. The plans for the playing field were to echo the current ball yard with a 37-foot left-field wall with a manual scoreboard, a short poke in right, bullpens in front of the right-field bleachers and a center-field triangle. The park would also have included a cantilevered upper deck with thousands of new seats far more remote than any in old Fenway and the virtual banishment of outside vendors. "Building a new ballpark is not an optional choice for the Red Sox or any other ballpark, but a necessity," said general manager Dan Duquette. The new Fenway never got off the ground, however. In March 2005, the Red Sox announced that they were no longer pursuing a new facility and would remain at Fenway Park for the foreseeable future.

# 16
## May

**M**aking his first two starts of the 1954 season on this date, Ted Williams collected eight hits, including two homers and a double, in nine at-bats during a double-header against the Tigers in Detroit. He had been out of action since March 1 when he broke his collarbone during a spring training workout. Grimacing in pain with every swing, Williams was 3-for-4 in the first game and 5-for-5 in the second tilt. He also drove in eight runs during the twin bill, six of them in the nightcap. The Tigers won both games, however. Williams hit .345 with 29 homers in 117 games and 386 at-bats in 1954. Under the rules then in force, a player needed 400 at-bats to qualify for the batting title. Bobby Avila of the Indians was awarded the crown with a .341 mark. There was some controversy over the 1954 AL batting championship because Williams failed to accumulate the required number of official at-bats, in part because he drew 136 walks. A change was made in 1957 in which plate appearances were the basis for qualifying for the batting title. A player needed 3.1 plate appearances per scheduled game. Williams had more than enough plate appearances under that criteria in 1954, but the rule wasn't retroactive, and Avila still holds the AL batting title.

**B**

**17**
**May**

**O**n this date in 1971, the Red Sox signed Luis Tiant following his release by the Braves. This proved to be one of the best moves ever made by the club. Among pitchers in club history, he ranks fifth in wins (123), fourth in games started (238), fourth in shutouts (26), fourth in innings pitched (1,774⅔), fifth in strikeouts (1,075) and sixth in complete games (113). Tiant had a lifetime record of 82-67 when acquired by the Sox that included a 1968 season in which he was 21-9 with a 1.60 ERA while pitching for the Indians. But he was at least 30 years old (his exact age is open to speculation), and nearly every club in the majors considered him washed up. Luis was overweight and recovering from a broken clavicle that doctors concluded would heal only with rest. The acquisition didn't look like much from the start. In June 1972, he had been in Boston for more than a year and his record with the Sox was a dismal 1-9. Suddenly in mid-season in 1972, Tiant regained his touch and became one of the best pitchers in baseball. He was 15-6 in 1972, 20-13 in 1973, 22-13 in 1974, 18-15 in 1975 and 22-12 in 1976. With his trademark whirling-dervish pitching wind-up that began with his back to the batter, Cuban-born Tiant became one of the most popular players ever to play for the Red Sox.

# 18
## May

On this date in 1986, Red Sox center fielder Steve Lyons was having a bad day at Fenway Park. He made an error that cost a run, overthrew a cutoff man, messed up a sacrifice bunt, got picked off, and ran to the wrong base. Strangely, his base-running error led to the victory of the Sox over the Rangers, 5-4 in 10 innings. Lyons was on second base in the 10th with the Sox trailing 4-3 and one out. Marty Barrett blooped a double down the right-field line that eluded Texas outfielder George Wright, who dove for the ball and held it momentarily before it popped loose. As Lyons approached third, he looked back and thought the ball had been caught. He headed back to second and arrived at the same time as Barrett. Not believing what he saw, Wright began running the ball toward the infield as Lyons took off for third again. Wright threw to the bag, but the toss was wide. Pitcher Greg Harris backed up the play, but the ball went threw his legs and into the dugout. The two-base error allowed both Lyons and Barrett to score to give the Sox the 5-4 decision.

**19**
**May**

**O**n this date in 2008, Jon Lester pitched a no-hitter to defeat the Royals 7-0 at Fenway Park. He threw 130 pitches, walked two and struck out nine. In the ninth inning, Lester walked Esteban German, then retired Tony Pena on a ground out to third baseman Mike Lowell, David DeJesus on a grounder unassisted to first baseman Kevin Youkilis, and Alberto Callaspo on a strikeout swinging. The no-hitter was part of a remarkable comeback for Lester. As a 22-year-old rookie in 2006, Lester was diagnosed in September with a treatable form of anaplastic large-cell lymphoma. The disease went into remission, and he began pitching again for the Red Sox in July 2007. Lester started and won the clinching fourth game of the 2007 World Series against the Rockies. In addition, Jason Varitek set a record by catching his fourth no-hitter. He was also behind the plate for no-hitters by Hideo Nomo in 2001, Derek Lowe in 2002 and Clay Buchholz in 2007.

# 20
## May

O n this date in 1976, Bill Lee was injured in a vicious brawl during an 8-2 win over the Yankees in New York. The fight started in the sixth inning when Lou Piniella crashed into Carlton Fisk in a play at the plate. Fisk held onto the ball for the out, then jumped on Piniella, who was stretched out at the plate. The dugouts emptied, and fights broke out everywhere. Lee came in from the mound firing punches and was sucker-punched by Mickey Rivers in the back of the head. Lee ended up under one pile, and after he got up, was grabbed by Graig Nettles. The two began throwing punches at one another. Nettles lifted Lee off the ground and slammed him shoulder-first into the ground. Lee chased Nettles around the field shouting obscenities, and Nettles dropped him with another punch to the eye. Lee suffered torn ligaments in his pitching shoulder. In a press conference the following day, Lee called Yankee manager Billy Martin a "Nazi" and referred to the Yankees as "Steinbrenner's Brown Shirts." Lee didn't pitch again until July and was rarely effective, finishing the season with a 5-7 record and a 5.63 ERA. The next meeting of the two brawling teams was at Fenway Park on May 31. The umpires threatened a forfeit after a cherry bomb exploded in front of Rivers in the eighth inning. The Sox lost 8-3.

**21
May**

**O**n this date in 1977, the Red Sox scored four runs in the ninth inning to defeat the Brewers 10-9 at Fenway Park. The rally started with a long homer by Jim Rice that struck the center-field wall behind the bleachers. An RBI double by George Scott pulled the Sox within a run. After a walk to Carlton Fisk, Dwight Evans hit a single that scored Scott to tie it at 9-9 and send Fisk to third. Butch Hobson grounded to Don Money at second base for a forceout, but Evans's takeout slide prevented the Brewers from completing a double play and allowed Fisk to score the winning run.

# 22
## May

**D**own 10-7 on this date in 1977, the Red Sox scored seven runs in the eighth inning to beat the Brewers 14-10 in the first game of a double-header at Fenway Park. George Scott broke the 10-10 tie with a grand slam off Rick Folkers. The game produced 11 homers in all, six by the Red Sox. In addition to Scott's home run, Fred Lynn hit a pair, and Carl Yastrzemski, Butch Hobson and Dwight Evans added one each. Evans's homer cleared the center-field wall about 20 feet to the right of the flagpole. Don Money hit two for Milwaukee, and Sixto Lezcano, Mike Hegan and Von Joshua hit one apiece. The Red Sox' bats went silent in the second game as the Brewers won 6-0.

**23 May**

On this date in 1978, the American League owners approved the sale of the club by the Yawkey estate to a group headed by Jean Yawkey, Haywood Sullivan and Buddy LeRoux. Yawkey remained as club president with LeRoux serving as vice-president of administration and Sullivan as vice-president and general manager. From the start, LeRoux and Sullivan squabbled. The new ownership pinched pennies and was indecisive, which crippled the club's ability to win a pennant. Yawkey was supposed to be a silent partner. Her cash was needed to obtain the approval of the sale for the AL owners, and as the widow of the beloved Tom Yawkey, who died in 1976, her inclusion was good public relations. Yawkey insisted on giving her opinion on major decisions, however, and when Sullivan and LeRoux disagreed over the direction of the club, she aligned with Sullivan. Lines of authority were constantly blurred, and employees were caught between two warring factions and were afraid of making decisions for fear of alienating one of the three principal owners. LeRoux sold his shares in 1987, but eventually Sullivan too fell out of favor with Mrs. Yawkey. The ownership muddle wasn't completely resolved until well into the 1990s.

## 24
### May

**J**immy Piersall and Billy Martin engaged in a vicious fight on this date in 1952 before a 5-2 Red Sox win over the Yankees at Fenway Park. Piersall and Martin had been riding each other all spring. Before the May 24 game, Martin was warming up on the sideline while Piersall took fielding practice at shortstop when they began exchanging insults. Martin invited Piersall to meet him under the stands, where he dropped Piersall with two punches. Pitcher Ellis Kinder and coach Oscar Melillo of the Red Sox and coach Bill Dickey of the Yankees were hit in the head trying to break up the battle. Piersall went into the clubhouse and became involved in another fight with teammate Mickey McDermott.

# 25
## May

**O**n this date in 1984, the Red Sox traded Dennis Eckersley and Mike Brumley to the Cubs for Bill Buckner. The fates of both Buckner and Eckersley would have likely been much different if this trade had never ocurred. The Red Sox were desperate for a first baseman who could hit; the club had been trying to make do with Dave Stapleton at the position since 1980. Buckner was 34 when he arrived in Boston and wasn't much of a power hitter, with 119 career home runs in 6,683 at-bats, but had a .295 lifetime batting average. In five seasons with the Red Sox, from 1984 through 1987 and again in 1990, he batted .279 with 48 homers in 526 games. Eckersley hadn't pitched well for years; he seemed to be washed up at the age of 29 when he was shipped to Chicago. In 1983 and 1984, he pitched 241 innings for the Sox and was 13-17 with a 5.45 ERA. Eckersley pitched well in spots for the Cubs before they traded him to the Athletics in 1986. There, he was converted from a starter to a reliever and became one of the most dominant closers in the history of the game. From 1988 through 1992, Eckersley saved 220 games and had an ERA of 1.93 in 354 innings. He played for the Red Sox again in 1998, the 24th and last year of his career. Eckersley was elected to the Hall of Fame in 2004, the first year he appeared on the ballot.

# 26
## May

**T**he question of the day.
How did the last episode of *Cheers* affect the Red Sox?
On May 19, 1993, the night before the airing of the last episode of *Cheers*, John Ratzenberger threw out the ceremonial first pitch before a 10-5 win over the Blue Jays. Ratzenberger played know-it-all postal employee Cliff Clavin on the series. The actor threw the ball over the head of Tony Pena. Later, Ratzenberger helped the grounds crew rake the infield. The following night, the Sox started the game against the Blue Jays at 6:05 p.m., 90 minutes earlier than usual, so that it would not interfere with the airing of the final episode, scheduled to begin at 9:20 p.m. The 4-3 loss drew 18,219, the only crowd at Fenway Park under 20,000 all year. During the 11-year run of the series, there was a constant tie-in with the Red Sox because the fictional lead character, Sam Malone, played by Ted Danson, was portrayed as a former pitcher with the club. Actor Nicholas Colasanto's character, Ernie Pantusso, was an ex-coach for the Sox. Colasanto died after the end of season three. Red Sox players Luis Tiant and Wade Boggs made guest appearnces on the show.

**27 May**

**O**n this date in 1986, the Sox were leading 2-1 against the Indians in the botoom of the sixth at Cleveland's Municipal Stadium when the game had to be called because of fog from Lake Erie. Tony Armas made a remarkable catch to save the game. With two runners on base, Mel Hall hit a shot into the fog. Armas saw it off the bat, guessed where it was going to land, ran back to the fence and caught it out of sight of almost everyone in the ballpark, perhaps even the umpires. After the game, Oil Can Boyd noted, "That's what you get when you build a ballpark by the ocean."

# 28
## May

**T**he question of the day.

When did the Red Sox play their first night game at Fenway Park?

The first night game in big-league history took place in 1935 between the Reds and Phillies at Crosley Field in Cincinnati. By the end of the 1946 season, 13 of the 16 teams in the majors were playing a portion of their home schedule at night. The three holdouts were the Red Sox, Tigers and Cubs. Tom Yawkey finally decided to install lights in 1947. The first night game at Fenway took place on June 13 with the Red Sox defeating the White Sox 5-3 before 34,510. Night games proved to be a tremendous success, as the Red Sox drew 463,822 in 14 nocturnal tilts, an average of 33,130. The 12 double-headers in 1947 averaged 20,799, and the 43 single day games averaged 16,602. The Tigers began hosting night games in 1948. The Cubs held out until 1988 before installing lights at Wrigley Field.

**29**
**May**

**T**he question of the day.
Who is the only Red Sox
player to score a touchdown in
the Rose Bowl?

Outfielder Jackie Jensen played for
the Red Sox from 1954 through 1959
and again in 1961. He was a football
star at the University of California, where
he scored on a 67-yard touchdown run
in the 1949 Rose Bowl. Jensen's wife was Zoe
Ann Olsen, who won the silver and bronze medals in the 1948 and
1952 Olympics as a springboard diver. Both were athletic, blond
and good-looking and were called "the world's most famous sweet-
hearts." There were 1,000 guests at their 1949 wedding reception.

# 30
## May

**O**n this date in 1913, Harry Hooper led off the first inning of both games of a double-header against the Senators in Washington with a home run. He is the only player in major league history to hit two lead-off homers in one day. Hooper hit a total of only four homers in 148 games during the 1913 season. He played right field for the Red Sox from 1909 through 1920 and was elected to the Hall of Fame in 1971. Before entering professional baseball, Hooper earned a civil engineering degree from St. Mary's College in Oakland, California. He signed with the Red Sox after hitting .344 in 1908 for Sacramento in the California League. The Sox offered Hooper $2,500 to sign, but as a California native, he was reluctant to leave the West Coast. Boston owner John I. Taylor sweetened the deal by offering him $2,850 and promised him a job working on the design of the new ballpark he was planning. Hooper was never asked to contribute to the design of Fenway Park, however. He made a significant contribution on the field with his speed and powerful right arm. Hooper is the only player in Red Sox history to compete in four World Series for the club, playing in 1912, 1915, 1916 and 1918.

**31**
**May**

On this date in 1970, the Red Sox lost to the White Sox 22-13 at Fenway Park in the third-highest scoring game in American League history. The record was set on June 29, 1950, when the Red Sox defeated the Athletics 22-14 in Philadelphia and tied on August 12, 2008, when the Sox edged the Rangers 19-17 at Fenway. There were 40 hits in the Red Sox–White Sox clash, including 11 doubles, two triples and three homers. Red Sox starter Gary Peters allowed six runs in the first inning. It was the first of two games between the two clubs in 1970 in which at least 30 runs were scored. On August 30, the Red Sox collected 22 hits and defeated the White Sox 21-11 in the first game of a double-header at Fenway. The Red Sox scored eight runs in the second inning and led 13-10 at the end of the fourth. A more conventional 4-1 victory in the second tilt completed the sweep of Chicago.

**B**

# June

# B

**01**
**June**

**O**n this date in 1935, Red Sox coach Al Schacht broke up a fight in a novel way during a 6-0 win over the Yankees in New York. In the fifth inning, Boston outfielder Roy Johnson was hit on the head by a pitch from Johnny Allen. Johnson started for the pitcher, but members of both teams came between them. Then Schacht put on a burlesque fight in which he knocked himself out and turned the whole affair into a joke. While a respected pitching coach, Schacht, who coached the Sox in 1934 and 1935, is best known for his side-splitting pantomime comedy routines, which he performed at 25 World Series and 18 All-Star Games and earned him the nickname "The Clown Prince of Baseball."

# 02
## June

**O**n this date in 1902, the Red Sox tied major league records for most runs scored in the ninth inning with two out and no one on base (nine) and for most consecutive hits (10) during a 13-2 trouncing of the Brewers in Milwaukee. Each of the 10 hits came off Bill Reidy and included four singles, five doubles and Freddy Parent's first major league home run. Boston accomplished the rally without star players Jimmy Collins and Buck Freeman, who were both ejected by umpire John Haskell in the fourth inning. In 1901, American League rosters only had 14 players. The tossings forced left fielder Tommy Dowd to move to third base for the first time in six years, put pitcher Nig Cuppy in left field and placed another pitcher, Ben Beville, at first base. Beville, whose career in the majors lasted three games, had both of his big-league hits in the game. The 10 consecutive hits came from Cuppy, Beville, Parent, Hobe Ferris, Ossie Schreckengost, Cy Young, Dowd, Charlie Hemphill, Chick Stahl and Cuppy again.

**B**

**03**
**June**

**D**utch Leonard pitched his second career no-hitter on this date in 1918 to defeat the Tigers 5-0 in Detroit. The only base runner that Leonard allowed was Bobby Veach, who drew a walk with two out in the first inning. Front that point forward, Leonard set down 25 batters in a row. In the ninth, he began by retiring Archie Yelle on a grounder to Everett Scott at short. Ty Cobb, out of the starting lineup with an injured shoulder, pinch-hit and fouled out to third baseman Fred Thomas. Donie Bush ended the game as Leonard's fourth strikeout victim. Leonard pitched his first no-hitter on August 30, 1916. The day before, he failed to survive the first inning in a start against the Browns at Fenway Park. Sent back to the mound without a day of rest, Leonard set down the first 23 Browns he faced, struck out three, and walked two in the no-hitter. In the ninth, he retired Doc Lavan, walked Grover Hartley and induced Burt Shotton and Jack Tobin to hit fly balls for the last two outs of the game.

# 04
## June

**O**n this date in 1989, the Red Sox blew a 10-run lead and lost 13-11 in 12 innings to the Blue Jays at Fenway Park. It is the largest blown lead in franchise history in a loss. The Sox also blew a 10-run lead and fell behind on August 12, 2008, against the Rangers, but rallied to win 19-17 The Sox took a 10-0 advantage over Toronto with two runs in the sixth inning, but the Jays scored two in the seventh, four in the eighth and five in the ninth, the last four on a one-out grand slam by Ernie Whitt, to move ahead 11-10. The Sox sent the game into extra innings with a tally in the ninth, before the Blue Jays scored twice in the 12th on a homer by Junior Felix for the win. The pitchers who surrendered the lead were Mark Smithson, Bob Stanley, Ron Murphy, Lee Smith and Dennis Lamp.

**05**
**June**

**T**he Red Sox hammered the White Sox 17-1 on this date in 1929 at Fenway Park. Nine of Boston's 24 hits came consecutively with two out in the eight-run eighth inning. The nine straight hits came from Russ Scaritt, Bill Barrett, Bob Barrett (no relation), Phil Todt, Grant Gillis, Charlie Berry, Danny McFayden, Bill Narleski and Jack Rothrock. The inning ended when Rothrock was thrown out at second base trying to stretch a single into a double. Dan Dugan allowed the first eight hits. Rothrock's hit was surrendered by 42-year-old White Sox manager Lena Blackburne, who was so disgusted with the performance that he took the mound himself. It was the last time that Blackburne played during his 548-game big-league career, and it was his only appearance as a pitcher.

# 06
## June

**T**his day in 1983 was an eventful day for the Boston Red Sox. They staged "Tony Conigliaro Night" at Fenway Park. The net proceeds from the game were earmarked to help defray Conigliaro's staggering medical costs following his 1982 heart attack, which left him in a coma. Earlier in the day, the Sox selected Roger Clemens with the first pick of the amateur draft. The biggest news on June 6, 1983, however, wasn't "Tony Conigliaro Night" or the drafting of Clemens, but majority partner Buddy LeRoux's attempted takeover of the club. LeRoux rocked the organization by calling a press conference to announce that his partnership with Jean Yawkey and Haywood Sullivan had been reorganized. After feuding with Yawkey and Sullivan for years, LeRoux said he teamed with the minority partners and that he was in charge. LeRoux also said that Sullivan was out as general manager and was being replaced by Dick O'Connell. Sullivan called a press conference of his own and said that LeRoux's takeover was illegal and that he was in charge. In effect, the Sox had two owners and two general managers. LeRoux lost his case in court in 1984 and sold his shares to Yawkey and Sullivan in 1987.

**07**
**June**

On this date in 1942, the Red Sox won an exciting double-header against the White Sox, both by 3-2 scores, at Fenway Park. In the first game, Bobby Doerr and Jim Tabor both hit home runs in the ninth inning to erase a 2-1 Chicago lead. The Red Sox scored a run in the eighth inning of the second tilt to take a 3-2 advantage. Because of the Sunday sports law, the game had to end precisely at 6:30 p.m. With that time approaching, White Sox manager Jimmy Dykes tried to prolong the contest as long as possible. If the eighth inning didn't end before 6:30, the entire inning would be wiped out, and the game would go into the books as a 2-2 tie. With the crowd in an uproar, Dykes changed pitchers three times and was prevented from making a fourth change only because the umpires threatened a forfeit. Eventually, the inning ended before the appointed time, and the Red Sox were winners.

# 08
## June

**T**he Red Sox set a club record for most runs in a game on this date in 1950 with a 29-4 trouncing of the Browns at Fenway Park. The 25-run winning margin is also a club record. Boston scored eight runs in the second inning, five in the third, seven in the fourth, two in the fifth, two in the seventh and five in the eighth. The 28-hit attack included nine doubles, one triple and seven homers. Bobby Doerr hit three home runs and Ted Williams and Walt Dropo each added two. Boston also set major league records for most total bases in a game (60) and most extra base hits (17). Combined with a 20-4 win over the Browns the previous day, the Sox set a major league record for most runs in consecutive games with 49. Other modern (since 1900) records included most hits in consecutive games (51), most players scoring at least three runs in a game (seven) and an American League record for most players with four or more hits (four). Al Zarilla tied a major league record for most doubles with four and also hit a single. Zarilla, Johnny Pesky and Clyde Vollmer tied a modern record for most plate appearances in a nine-inning game with eight. Chuck Stobbs tied a record for most base on balls by a pitcher with four.

**B**

**09**
June

On this date in 1946, the Red Sox extended their winning streak to 10 games with a 7-1 and 11-6 sweep of the Tigers in a double-header at Fenway Park. Boo Ferriss was the winning pitcher in the second game, which gave him a record of 10-0 on the season. Ted Williams hit one of the longest home runs ever at Fenway in the first inning of the second game. It landed in row 33 of the bleachers and struck construction worker Joe Boucher on the head, knocking a hole in his straw hat. The homer is still marked today by a single red seat amid the green.

**B**

# 10
## June

**O**n this date in 1938, Red Sox pitcher Bill LeFebvre clubbed a home run over the Green Monster on the first pitch of his first major league at-bat. He hit it off Monty Stratton of the White Sox at Fenway Park. LeFebvre was less effective on the mound, however, allowing six runs in four innings of a 15-2 loss. He made his major league debut just days after graduating from Holy Cross College, where his baseball coach was former Red Sox manager Jack Barry. LeFebvre was soon back in the minors and didn't appear in another big-league game until the following season. He played in 75 games in the majors and never hit another homer, but batted a respectable .276 in 87 at-bats. With the Senators in 1944, he had 29 at-bats as a pinch-hitter and led the American League with 10 pinch-hits. On the mound, LeFebvre ended his career with a 5-5 record and a 5.03 ERA. The only other Red Sox players with homers in their first major league at-bats are Eddie Pellagrini in 1946 and Bob Tillman in 1962. LeFebvre is the only one of the three to do it on the first pitch.

**B**

# 11
## June

**W**il Cordero was arrested on this date in 1997 for assaulting his wife Ana in the their Cambridge apartment. According to the police report, Cordero slapped his wife, hit her with a phone when she attempted to call for help, and threatened to kill her. Ana emerged with a bloody nose and bruises. Some in the Red Sox front office supported Cordero, while other wanted to hang him from the nearest lamppost, leading to indecisiveness and inaction. The Sox reluctantly bowed to community pressure and suspended Cordero for two weeks, brought him back, then benched him again when his wife made more allegations. Later, he shrugged off the incident during an ESPN interview in which he denied he had a problem. Cordero finished the season under a cloud and a torrent of boos whenever he stepped to the plate. He was released in September. Cordero received a suspended sentence when he pleaded to a lesser crime to avoid jail time. During his 14-year big-league career (1992–2005), Cordero played for eight different teams.

**12**
**June**

**T**he question of the day.

What major league team has scored the most runs in a season since 1937?

The 1950 Red Sox scored 1,027 runs and had a batting average of .302. Both are the highest of any major league club from 1937 through the present. The starting lineup consisted of Birdie Tebbetts (c), Walt Dropo (1b), Bobby Doerr (2b), Johnny Pesky (3b), Vern Stephens (ss), Ted Williams (lf), Dom DiMaggio (cf) and Al Zarilla (rf). In addition, Billy Goodman won the batting title with a .354 average by playing in 110 games as a utility player. He played a key role by filling in as a left fielder when Ted Williams was out for two months with a broken elbow. Goodman had never previously played in the outfield. None of the nine regulars batted lower than .294. Three drove in 120 runs or more. Five scored at least 100 runs and seven scored at least 90. Boston finished the year in third place, four games out of first, with a 94-60 record, however, because the pitching staff had trouble stopping anyone.

## 13
### June

**T**he question of the day.

How did an injury to Carney Lansford change the history of the Red Sox?

Carney Lansford severely sprained his ankle on a play at the plate while trying for an inside-the-park home run on June 23, 1982. The injury changed the history of the Red Sox because it gave Wade Boggs a chance to play regularly while Lansford was recuperating. When the season began, Boggs was a 23-year-old rookie. He had hit over .300 in each of his five seasons in the minors, but the Red Sox didn't consider him to be a solid major league prospect. The club hierarchy believed that he lacked the power to play first base and that he didn't have the defensive skills to play third. During the first 65 games of the 1982 season, Boggs was one of the last options off the Red Sox bench. He appeared in just 14 games and had only 29 at-bats and a .241 batting average. After being inserted into the lineup for Lansford, Boggs immediately proved his worth by hitting .349 over the course of the season in 104 games, although as late as August, manager Ralph Houk still wasn't convinced Boggs could play effectively on a daily basis. Fortunately, the Sox came to their senses and traded Lansford during the following off-season and installed Boggs as the starter at third.

**B**

# 14
## June

**O**n this date in 1949, the Red Sox allowed the Indians to use a "courtesy runner" in the first inning of a 10-5 loss at Fenway Park. Lou Boudreau was hit on the elbow by a pitch and was taken to the dressing room for treatment. The man who went in to run for Boudreau was Ken Keltner, who was already in the game and had scored earlier in the inning. While serving as a runner for Boudreau, Keltner scored again and was credited with two runs scored in the inning. Boudreau returned to the game in the second inning.

**B**

**15 June**

**O**n this date in 1976, the Red Sox purchased Rollie Fingers and Joe Rudi from the Athletics for $2 million. On the same day, the Yankees bought Vida Blue from the A's for $1.5 million. Almost immediately, baseball commissioner Bowie Kuhn questioned the big-money deals and indicated that he might void the sales. Kuhn dictated that the three players remain on the Oakland active roster until he reached a decision, but the three could not participate in any games. Before Kuhn issued the edict, Rudi and Fingers were in Red Sox uniforms for a game against the Tigers. Fingers threw in the bullpen late in the game. Rudi was available for pinch-hit duty, but manager Darrell Johnson kept him on the bench. On June 18, Kuhn canceled the transaction "in the best interest of baseball." Kuhn feared that the sale of players for such large amounts of cash would adversely affect "the public's confidence in baseball" by upsetting the game's "competitive balance." The Red Sox were outraged by Kuhn's verdict. "Who do we check with now if we want to buy a player?" general manager Dick O'Connell asked. "Who determines if his batting average is low enough or if the price is low enough?" Rudi and Fingers became free agents at the end of the season. Rudi signed with the Angels, and Fingers signed with the Padres. Rudi later played for the Sox in 1981.

# 16
## June

**O**n this date in 1938, Jimmie Foxx tied a major league record by drawing six walks in six plate appearances during a 12-8 win over the Browns in St. Louis. Foxx swung at only two pitches during the afternoon. The Browns pitchers walked a total of eight batters during the game. Foxx drew three walks from Ed Tietje, one from Ed Linke and two from Russ Van Atta. The only other major leaguer with six walks in a nine-inning game is Walt Wilmot of the Chicago Cubs in 1891. Foxx was suffering from sinus trouble that day, and it affected his vision. Because he couldn't see the pitches clearly, he simply let most sail by. Foxx nearly didn't play, but his potential replacements at first base were injured. In June 1939, Foxx was hospitalized with sinus trouble. His aliment led to a unique addition to Fenway Park. In order to protect Foxx from the glare of the sun, a canvas curtain was designed for use in the back section of the grandstand running behind the third base line. The screen was 25 feet long and 15 feet high and hung from a heavy wire.

**B**

**17**
**June**

On this date in 1943, Bunker Hill Day, player-manager Joe Cronin hit a three-run pinch-homer in each game of a double-header against the Athletics at Fenway Park. In the first game, Cronin inserted himself into the game batting for Lou Lucier with the Sox trailing 4-1 in the seventh inning with two runners on base. He tied the score with a homer off Russ Christopher, and the Red Sox went on to win 5-4 with a run in the ninth. In the second tilt, Cronin pinch-hit for Mike Ryba and hit another homer with two on base in the eighth, facing Don Black. The Red Sox lost 8-7. Cronin had hit another three-run, pinch-hit homer against the Athletics two days earlier. He had five pinch-hit homers during the 1943 season, which still stands as the American League record. They were also the only five pinch-hit homers of Cronin's 20-year career. Overall, he was 18-for-42 as a pinch-hitter in 1943, a batting average of .429.

# 18
## June

**O**n this date in 1953, the Red Sox set a modern major league record for most runs in an inning by scoring 17 times in the seventh inning of a 23-3 victory over the Tigers at Fenway Park. The Chicago Cubs were the only other big-league team to score more in an inning, with 18 on September 18, 1883. The Sox sent 23 batters to the plate in 47 minutes against Detroit pitcher Steve Gromek, Dick Weik and Earl Harrist. Boston banged out 14 hits to set an American League mark for a single inning and had 27 hits in the game on 23 singles, two doubles and two homers. Gene Stephens had three hits in the big inning on two singles and a double to tie a major league record. The outburst came in a season in which he batted .204 in 221 at-bats. Sammy White tied a record by scoring three runs of the 17 runs. He was one of 11 to cross the plate in the inning, including a pinch-hitter and pinch-runner. The others to score were Tom Umphlett, Stephens, George Kell, Jimmy Piersall, Dick Gernert, Billy Goodman, Ellis Kinder, Johnny Lipon, Al Zarilla and Ted Lepcio. Zarilla pinch-hit for Piersall, who had been taken out of the game by manager Lou Boudreau for exchanging insults with Detroit catcher Matt Batts. Combined with a 17-1 win on June 17, the Sox outscored the Tigers 40-4 in back-to-back games.

**B**

**19**
**June**

**O**n this date in 1977, Carl Yastrzemski hit the longest known home run to the right of the Fenway Park bleachers. It reached approximately 460 feet before striking the facing of the right-field roof to the right of where the retired number 42 now stands. It is the only ball ever to reach the right-field roof facade. From June 17 through 19, the Red Sox set a major league record for most home runs in three consecutive games with 16, all against the Yankees. During the June 17 contest, the Red Sox hit four home runs in the first inning, all off Catfish Hunter, including two by Rick Burleson and Fred Lynn to lead off the game. The Sox won the three games by scores of 9-4, 10-4 and 11-1. The 16 homers were struck by Yastrzemski (four), George Scott (three), Bernie Carbo (three), Carlton Fisk (two), Burleson (one), Lynn (one), Denny Doyle (one) and Jim Rice (one).

# 20
## June

**T**he question of the day.
When did the Red Sox start 18 different players during a double-header?

Manager Eddie Kasko employed two entirely different lineups during a double-header against the Yankees on September 6, 1971. No one played both games. The lineup in the opener was John Kennedy (2b), Luis Aparicio (ss), Carl Yastrzemski (lf), Reggie Smith (cf), Billy Conigliaro (rf), Mike Fiore (1b), Phil Gagliano (3b), Bob Montgomery (c) and Ray Culp (p). In the nightcap, the batting order consisted of Doug Griffin (2b), Rick Miller (cf), Joe Lahoud (rf), Rico Petrocelli (3b), George Scott (1b), Ben Oglivie (lf), Juan Beniquez (cf), Carlton Fisk (c) and John Curtis (p). There were no substitutes among the position players in either contest. Bill Lee relieved in the first game and Luis Tiant in the second. The shuffling did no good, as the Sox lost both ends of the twin bill, the first 3-2 in 10 innings and the second 5-3. The day before, Kasko was given a two-year extension on his contract through 1973. Two days prior, player Rico Petrocelli publicly stated that Kasko was responsible for the club's failure to win the pennant in 1971. Petrocelli said Kasko showed favoritism, did nothing to promote team unity and caused the club to break into factions.

**21**
**June**

On this date in 1938, Red Sox third baseman Pinky Higgins set a major league record with hits in 12 consecutive at-bats. Higgins had eight hits in eight at-bats on this day during a double-header against the Tigers in Detroit, in which the Red Sox won 8-3 and lost 5-4. The streak began on June 19 when Higgins hit a single in his last at-bat during a 3-2 loss to the White Sox in the first game of a double-header in Chicago. In the second game, he was 3-for-3 in a 6-1 Boston win. The Red Sox were idle on June 20. The streak ended when Higgins went hitless in four at-bats facing Vern Kennedy of the Tigers. The only other major leaguer with hits in 12 consecutive at-bats is Walt Dropo of the Tigers in 1952. Higgins later managed the Red Sox from 1955 through 1962 and was the general manager from 1962 through 1965. In 1968, an intoxicated Higgins ran over and killed a Louisiana highway worker and injured three others. He was found guilty of negligent homicide and sentenced to four years of hard labor but was paroled after two months. Higgins died of a heart attack in 1969, two days after being released from jail.

# 22
## June

**T**he question of the day.
Which Red Sox hitter re-
ceived a letter of encouragement
from the President of the United
States?

In May and June of 1971, Luis
Aparicio suffered through a streak in
which he went hitless in 44 consecutive
at-bats and received a letter of encouragement from President Richard Nixon. "In my own
career," Nixon wrote, "I have experienced long periods when I
couldn't get a hit no matter how hard I tried, but in the end, I was
able to hit a home run." Aparicio was elected as the starting shortstop by the fans that season, even though he was hitting as low as
.151 in early June and .206 at the All-Star break.

**23**
**June**

On this date in 1917, Ernie Shore pitched a "perfect game" against the Senators to win 4-0 at Fenway Park. Babe Ruth was the starting pitcher and walked Washington leadoff batter Ray Morgan on four pitches. Ruth tersely disputed the calls of home-plate umpire Brick Owens and was ejected. The Babe responded to the banishment by rushing toward Owens. Catcher Pinch Thomas tried to intercept Ruth but was ineffective, and Ruth succeeded in swatting Owens on the neck. Thomas, who had a few choice words for Owens, was also ejected. Shore came on in relief, and after Morgan was caught stealing, recorded outs against all 26 batters he faced. In the ninth, Shore retired Howard Shanks, John Henry (on a running catch by Duffy Lewis in left field) and pinch-hitter Mike Menosky (on a pop-up to second baseman Jack Barry). Catcher Sam Agnew, who entered the game with Shore after Thomas was ejected, collected three hits in three at-bats. Shore's tremendous pitching effort has long been erroneously listed as a perfect game in many record books. Since Shore was a relief pitcher and there was one Washington base runner, it doesn't fit the criteria of absolute perfection. Ruth was suspended for nine days and fined $100 because of the incident.

**B**

# 24
## June

O n this date in 1911, owner John I. Taylor announced plans to build a new ballpark in the Fenway section of Boston that eventually became known as Fenway Park. The plot was owned by the Fenway Realty Company, in which the Taylor family was a large stockholder. Plans called for a steel-and-concrete grandstand, wooden bleachers in left field, a right-field pavilion and a large wooden bleacher in extreme right and center fields. As late as 1880, when the city was already 250 years old, the section around present-day Fenway Park was a saltwater marsh flooded with sewage that collected from the runoff of the Muddy River and Stony Brook. To fix the problem with the Muddy River and Stony Brook, a tidal gate was built to control the sewage problem, and more landfill created the Back Bay Fans and a new residential area called Fenway and Kenmore Square. This created real estate opportunities, and the Taylor family bought up much of the land and established the Fenway Realty Company. In part, the ballpark was constructed and named Fenway Park to promote this relatively new part of Boston and the Taylor's real estate holdings.

# 25
## June

On this date in 1959, the Tigers defeated the Red Sox 10-5 in the last major league game between two clubs with all-Caucasian rosters. The Red Sox didn't integrate until Pumpsie Green made his debut on July 21, 1959. The Tigers had an all-white team from May 13, 1959, when they sold Larry Doby to the White Sox, until the following September, when William Proctor was called up from the minors. The Kansas City Athletics had no black players from May 26, 1959, when Hector Lopez was dealt to the Yankees, through the end of the 1960 season. The 1960 A's were the last all-white team in major league history.

# 26
## June

**E**arl Wilson pitched a no-hitter on this date in 1962 to defeat the Angels 2-0 before 14,002 at Fenway Park. Wilson also hit a solo homer in the third inning off Bo Belinsky to give the Sox a 1-0 lead. Belinsky pitched a no-hitter of his own six weeks earlier. It was also Wilson's first major league shutout. He struck out five, walked four and retired the last 11 batters in order. In the ninth, Billy Moran led off for the Angels and hit a blooper into short left that shortstop Eddie Bressoud caught one-handed. Leon Wagner followed with a weak fly ball to Carl Yastrzemski in left. The final out was recorded on a liner to center that was caught by Gary Geiger 400 feet from home plate. The only other pitchers to hit a home run during a no-hitter are Wes Ferrell of the Indians in 1931, Jim Tobin of the Braves in 1944 and Rick Wise of the Phillies in 1971. Wise hit two homers during his no-hitter. Wilson struck 35 home runs during his career, 17 of them as a member of the Red Sox. He holds the all-time club record for home runs by a pitcher. Ferrell also hit 17 while playing for the Sox from 1934 through 1937, but one of them was as a pinch-hitter. Babe Ruth hit 15 home runs for the Red Sox in games in which he appeared as a pitcher. Wilson also became the Red Sox first African-American pitcher when he debuted in 1959.

**27 June**

**R**ed Sox first baseman Harry Agganis died suddenly on this date in 1955 at the age of 26 at Sancta Maria Hospital in Cambridge, Massachusetts, of a massive pulmonary embolism caused by a blood clot in his leg that shot into his lung. Agganis had been in the hospital since June 5 with pneumonia and seemed to be recovering. His death came without warning. Known as the Golden Greek, Agganis was a native of Lynn, Massachusetts. He had a brilliant sports career at Boston University, where he starred in both football and baseball. Agganis was the number-one draft choice of the Cleveland Browns with the idea that he would succeed legendary future Pro Football Hall of Famer Otto Graham at quarterback. Agganis passed up football to sign with the Red Sox in 1952. He reached the majors in 1954 and hit .251 with 11 homers as a rookie. In 1955, he batted .313 in 25 games and seemed to be on the verge of greatness before succumbing to illness. Gaffney Street, on the Boston University campus and adjacent to the former site of Braves Field, was renamed Harry Agganis Way in 1995. The school also dedicated Harry Agganis Arena in 2004. A statute of Agganis stands outside the building. The athletic stadium at Camp Lejeune in North Carolina, where he served with the Marines, and a public square in Lynn are also named in his honor.

# 28
## June

**W**ith the Red Sox leading 9-4 in the eighth inning against the Orioles in Baltimore on this date in 1902, Orioles manager John McGraw was ejected after disputing a call. After McGraw refused to leave the field, umpire Tom Connolly awarded the game to the Red Sox by forfeit. Red Sox player-manager Jimmy Collins collected five hits in five at-bats. American League President Ban Johnson suspended McGraw indefinitely as a result of the forfeit, an act that would have major repercussions. McGraw bolted from the Orioles and the American League and signed to manage the New York Giants on July 9, a job he held until 1932. McGraw convinced most of the Orioles players to sign National League contracts, and by July 17, Baltimore was reduced to five able bodies. At the end of the season, the Baltimore franchise moved to New York, thereby creating the Red Sox' most-hated rival—the New York Yankees. McGraw remained bitter toward Johnson and the American League for years, and after the Giants won the 1904 NL pennant, McGraw refused to play the Red Sox in the World Series. It was the first of 10 pennants that he would win with the Giants in a 21-year span from 1904 through 1924.

# 29
## June

**O**n this date in 1950, the Red Sox outslugged the Athletics 22-14 in Philadelphia in the highest-scoring game in American AL history. There were 36 hits, 21 walks and one home run. Ted Williams drove in six of the runs. In the first inning, the Red Sox scored six runs and the Athletics four. In the second, Boston added nine runs, and Philadelphia countered with three to make the score 14-7. It was 15-7 at the end of the fourth, 16-8 after five, 18-9 after six, 20-12 after seven and 20-14 after eight before the Red Sox scored twice in the ninth. The contest stood alone as the record-setter until August 12, 2008, when the Red Sox and Rangers also combined for 36 runs during a 19-17 Boston triumph on a wild night at Fenway Park.

# 30
## June

**O**n this date in 1908, Cy Young pitched the third no-hitter of his career and his second with the Red Sox, to beat the Yankees 8-0 in New York. He also drove in four runs by hitting three singles. The only Yankee to reach base was Harry Niles, who walked leading off the first inning on a 3-2, then was caught stealing. Young retired the next 26 batters in a row. In the ninth inning, Young retired Wid Conroy on a leaping catch by Gavvy Cravath in left field, Walter Blair on a pop foul to catcher Lou Criger and Joe Lake on a grounder to Amby McConnell. Young struck out only two batters in the no-hitter while facing the minimum 27. At 41, Young is the oldest pitcher in major league history to throw a no-hitter, other than Nolan Ryan, who threw one at 43 and another at 44. Despite his age, Young had a marvelous season in 1908. He was 21-11 with a 1.26 ERA and 30 complete games.

**B**

July

B

# 01
## July

**O**n this date in 1901, Cy Young pitched a shutout and drove in the game's only run with a double to defeat the White Sox 1-0 in Chicago. It was the third 1-0 win for Young in a span of nine days. He is the only pitcher in major league history to earn 1-0 victories in three consecutive starts. It was Young's fourth consecutive shutout overall, starting with a 7-0 triumph over the Browns in Boston on June 13. Young beat the Tigers 1-0 on June 23 in Detroit, and the Browns 1-0 in St. Louis on June 28.

**02**
**July**

**T**he question of the day. How many All-Star Games have been played at Fenway Park?

There have been three All-Star Games at Fenway. The first was on July 9, 1946, with a 12-0 AL win. Ted Williams was the star of the game, with two homers, two singles and a walk in five plate appearances. He also drove in five runs. The second was played on July 31, 1961, and ended in a 1-1 tie after nine innings when heavy rain stopped play. The AL scored first on a first-inning homer by Rocky Colavito off Warren Spahn. The NL tied the score in the sixth on a two-out double by Bill White off Red Sox rookie Don Schwall. Jim Bunning and Camilo Pascual each pitched three hitless innings for the AL. Williams threw out the ceremonial first pitch before both the 1961 and 1999 All-Star Games. On July 13, 1999, the AL won 4-1 before 34,187 at Fenway. Pedro Martinez thrilled the hometown fans with two hitless innings, fanning five, including the first four. The AL took a 2-0 lead in the first inning, and after the NL plated a run in the third, the AL added two in the fourth. No one hit a home run.

# 03
## July

On this date in 1940, the Red Sox won 12-11 in storybook fashion against the Athletics at Fenway Park. The A's led 8-0 early in the game and were still ahead 10-3 when the Red Sox scored three times in the eighth inning, mounting the rally after two were out and nobody was on base. Jim Tabor batted in all three runs with a homer, but Philadelphia scored a run in the ninth to move ahead 11-6. In the bottom of the inning, the Sox scored six times to win the game. The first five runs were the result of three singles, a walk and a three-run homer by Ted Williams that tied the score 11-11. Jimmie Foxx won the contest with a walk-off homer.

**04**
**July**

On this date in 1901, the Red Sox defeated the Orioles 10-2 and 8-3 at Huntington Grounds. In the second game, the Sox scored six runs in the eighth inning to take an 8-3 lead. The first two runs were scored on a home run by Jimmy Collins. Fans celebrated by shooting off firecrackers, firing pistols into the air and blowing horns. The racket so unnerved Baltimore pitcher Frank Foreman that he gave up four more runs. The behavior of the fans was typical of the period on Independence Day. The American Medical Association began tracking deaths suffered on July 4 in 1903 and were appalled by their findings. From 1903 through 1909, 1,360 Americans died on the holiday, an average of 170 per year with a peak of 213 in 1909, mostly from fireworks and firearms. Beginning in 1911, governmental agencies and newspapers began a campaign to urge Americans to practice a "Safe and Sane" Fourth of July holiday. Many cities and towns began to outlaw the toy pistols, fireworks and cannons used in the celebrations. The crusade spread rapidly, and the number of deaths dropped to 41 by 1912.

# 05
## July

On this date in 1958, the Red Sox missed out on a chance to beat the Yankees in New York because of the American League Saturday-night curfew, which stipulated that no game could continue past 11:59 p.m. The Red Sox scored two runs in the 11th inning to take a 5-3 lead when the clock struck 11:59. According to the rule, the score then reverted to the end of the previous full inning, and the contest went into the books as a 10-inning, 3-3 tie.

**06**
**July**

**T**he question of the day.

Who was Norm Zauchin?

In a completely unexpected performance on May 27, 1955, Red Sox rookie first baseman Norm Zauchin exploded for three homers and 10 RBIs during a 16-0 thrashing of the Senators at Fenway Park. Zauchin hit a two-run homer off Bob Porterfield in the first inning, a grand slam off Dean Stone in the second, a one-run double facing Ted Abernathy in the fourth and a three-run homer off Abernathy in the fifth. Zauchin struck out against Pedro Ramos in the seventh. Entering the game, Zauchin had only 98 big-league at-bats with one homer, five RBIs and a .208 average. He finished the 1955 season with 27 homers and 93 RBIs, but hit just .239 and led the league in strikeouts. Zauchin sat on the bench for most of the remainder of his career, which ended in 1959. Zauchin's baseball career was instumental in meeting his wife, which happened in an unusual fashion. While playing in the minors in Birmingham in 1950, he chased a foul pop into the stands and landed in the lap of an attractive woman named Janet Mooney. He got her name from an usher and asked her out on a date. They were married two years later.

# 07
## July

On this date in 1923, the Red Sox set a club record for most runs allowed in a single game. The Indians scored in every inning, collected 24 hits and won 27-3 in Cleveland. The Indians set a major league record in the sixth inning (since tied) by scoring 13 runs with two out. Red Sox reliever Lefty O'Doul allowed all 13 runs, a modern major league mark for most runs allowed by a pitcher in an inning. Manager Frank Chance kept O'Doul on the mound despite the shelling because he was angry the pitcher had returned to the hotel three hours after curfew the previous evening. O'Doul would have gotten the third out without a run being scored if center fielder Mike Menosky hadn't dropped a fly ball with the bases loaded. O'Doul gave up two doubles, five singles and six walks in the inning. He surrendered 16 runs, 11 hits and eight walks in three innings. O'Doul pitched in the majors with the Yankees and Red Sox from 1919 through 1923 and appeared in 34 games, all in relief, with an ERA of 4.87. After four seasons in the Pacific Coast League, he returned to the big leagues as a successful 31-year-old outfielder. In 970 career games, O'Doul batted .349, including a .398 average with the 1929 Phillies and two NL batting titles.

B

**08**
**July**

**O**n this date in 1941, Ted Williams hit a dramatic two-out, three-run, ninth-inning home run in the All-Star Game to lift the American League to a 7-5 win at Briggs Stadium in Detroit. Williams gave the AL a 1-0 advantage in the fourth with an RBI-double, but the NL led 5-2 in the eighth. Dom DiMaggio made it 5-3 in the bottom of the eighth by driving in his brother Joe with a single. With one out in the AL ninth, Claude Passeau of the Cubs loaded the bases on two singles and a walk. Joe DiMaggio hit into a force play at second base, which scored one run to make the score 5-4 and left runners on first and third. Williams brought both of them home with his home run that struck the front of the roof of the double-decked stands in right field. Williams bounded happily around the bases laughing and clapping his hands. A Red Sox pitcher was also the victim of a dramatic ninth-inning rally. On July 7, 1964, at Shea Stadium, Dick Radatz allowed four runs in the ninth, the last three on a walk-off home run by Johnny Callison of the Phillies, to lose 7-4. Radatz entered the game in the seventh inning and retired the National League in order in the seventh and eighth, four on strikeouts, before folding.

**B**

# 09
## July

On this date in 1914, the Red Sox purchased 19-year-old pitcher, Babe Ruth, along with pitcher Ernie Shore and catcher Ben Egan, from the Baltimore Orioles of the International League. The price for the three is open to speculation, but whatever the price, it was a tremendous bargain. Several other clubs had a chance to purchase Ruth before he was snared by the Red Sox but considered the price too steep. Joseph Lannin, who became sole owner of the Red Sox less than two months earlier, was willing to pay up to show fans that he would spend whatever it took to bring Boston another pennant. Ruth made his major league debut two days later, allowing three runs and eight hits in a starting assignment against the Indians at Fenway Park. Ruth was lifted in the seventh inning when Duffy Lewis pinch-hit for him. Lewis came around to score, and the Red Sox won 4-3 with Ruth as the winning pitcher. The Sox rarely used him in the starting rotation in 1914. He pitched only 23 innings, had a 2-1 record, posted a 3.91 ERA and spent about a month back in the minors with Providence. Ruth became part of the regular rotation in 1915 with an 18-8 record, 2.44 ERA and a team-leading four home runs (no one else had more than two) in 92 at-bats.

**10**
July

**O**n this date in 1986, Oil Can Boyd walked out on the Red Sox. His troubles began in spring training. Severe weight loss and liver trouble that was diagnosed as hepatitis sent him to the hospital for a brief period. Later, he was tardy for several workouts and exhibition games, resulting in a fine. On July 10, he went into an emotional tirade in the Red Sox clubhouse upon learning that he had not been selected for the All-Star team. At the time, he had a record of 11-6. Boyd was having financial troubles, and his contract called for a $25,000 bonus if he was an All-Star. He was also snubbed in the All-Star selections in 1985 when he was 11-7 at the break. After ripping off his uniform, Boyd littered the locker room with clothing, verbally assaulted manager John McNamara and many of his teammates, and threw a cup of soda at Kevin Romine before leaving Fenway Park. When he failed to report the next evening, the Red Sox suspended him and announced he would have to apologize to his teammates before being reinstated. He had an altercation with Boston police, was arrested on an outstanding speeding ticket, and checked himself into the hospital for what team officials said was "a comprehensive evaluation including testing for drugs." The club reinstated Boyd in August, and he finished the season with a 16-10 record and a 3.78 ERA.

# 11
## July

On this date in 1950, Ted Williams broke his elbow during the All-Star Game, which the National League won 4-3 in 14 innings at Comiskey Park. The injury happened in the first inning when Williams made a spectacular catch off a drive by Ralph Kiner, then put out his gloved hand to brace himself for the collision with the wall. The bones of the lower and upper arm took the force of the blow, smashing into each other, breaking seven bone chips from the elbow. Despite the continuous pain, Williams played until the ninth inning, even driving in a run with a single in the eighth, but X-rays taken the following day revealed the fracture. On July 13, surgeons removed the bone chips during a 75-minute operation. Williams didn't play again until September 15.

**12**
**July**

**A** crew from Paramount Pictures arrived at Fenway Park on this date in 1956 to film sequences for *Fear Strikes Out,* the movie based on the life of Jimmy Piersall. Piersall rose to the occasion by making two brilliant catches in center field, then put a Hollywood ending on the evening by hitting a two-run walk-off homer to beat the White Sox 3-1. *Fear Strikes Out* was released in theaters in March 1957 with Anthony Perkins portraying Piersall. Perkins received strong reviews for his dramatic portrayal of Piersall, but the actor's lack of athletic ability in baseball scenes strained the credibility of the film. Piersall himself hated the movie, particularly with regard to the depiction of his father, played by Karl Malden. Piersall believed the film was entirely too harsh on his father, who was portrayed as the source for Piersall's mental illness. Subsequent medical research over the past 50 years has revealed that Piersall's problems were likely inherited. His mother spent much of her adult life in and out of mental institutions.

**B**

# 13
## July

**O**n this date in 1919, Red Sox pitcher Carl Mays walked off the field after the second inning of a 14-9 loss against the White Sox in Chicago, blaming his teammates for lack of support. The Red Sox suspended Mays because of his actions and tried to trade him to the Yankees. American League president Ban Johnson told Sox owner Harry Frazee not to trade Mays while he was under suspension, but Frazee defied the order and completed the deal on July 30, receiving Allan Russell, Bob McGraw and $40,000 in return. Johnson refused to let Mays play for the Yankees, but the New York club obtained a restraining order preventing Johnson from interfering. The case made it to the New York State Supreme Court, and Mays remained a Yankee. He would have a combined record of 53-20 in 1920 and 1921 for the Yanks and finished his career with 207 wins and 126 losses, but he will be remembered for one pitch. On August 16, 1920, one of his submarine deliveries struck the Indians' Ray Chapman on the head, resulting in Chapman's death the following day. Among eligible players, Mays is the only pitcher since 1900 who has won at least 200 games with a winning percentage of .600 who is *not* in the Hall of Fame—a direct result of both his disagreeable disposition and Chapman's death.

**14**
July

**O**n this date in 1946, Ted Williams hit three homers and drove in eight runs to lead the Red Sox to an 11-10 win over the Indians in the first game of a double-header at Fenway Park. One of the homers was a grand slam off Steve Gromek. Williams also hit a single and scored four times. Cleveland player-manager Lou Boudreau tied a major league record with extra-base hits in the contest by collecting four doubles and a homer. The Red Sox completed the sweep with a 6-4 victory in the nightcap. Boudreau had a career game but wound up on the losing end of the score. In the second tilt, he deployed the famous "Boudreau shift" by moving his fielders to the right side of the diamond with only the left fielder on the left side, and he was positioned in left-center. Today, this is a common defense used against power hitters, but was a novel strategy in 1946. The Boudreau shift was soon copied by other AL clubs and used for several years. Williams refused to change his batting style by slicing hits to the opposite field, but the shifts failed to slow him down. Williams led the American League in batting average in 1947 and 1948, and missed a third consecutive crown in 1949 by one base hit.

# 15
## July

**O**n this date in 1986, Roger Clemens was the starting pitcher in the All-Star Game and thrilled the crowd at the Astrodome and the national television audience with three perfect innings. It was a homecoming for Clemens, who grew up in the Houston suburb of Katy. The NL came into the game with 26 wins in the previous 29 Midsummer Classics. Clemens was baseball's fastest-rising star, with a 14-0 start to the 1986 season and a 20-strikeout performance in April. He came into the All-Star Game with a 15-2 record. In setting down nine straight National Leaguers, Clemens struck out Ryne Sandberg and Darryl Strawberry. He was also the winning pitcher in a 3-2 AL victory. Clemens entered the 1986 season with a 16-9 lifetime record and a 3.88 ERA in two seasons cut short by injuries. He won the MVP Award and the first of six career Cy Young Awards that season with a 24-4 record and a 2.48 ERA. Clemens also started the All-Star Game in Houston again in 2004 as a member of the Astros at Minute Maid Park. He began the 2004 season, his first in the National League, with a 9-0 record and was 10-3 at the break. Clemens's second All-Star start didn't work out quite as well as the first, as he gave up five runs in an inning.

**B**

**16**
July

**T**he question of the day.

Who was Don Schwall?

Don Schwall looked like he might be headed for the Hall of Fame with a spectacular start as a 25-year-old rookie in 1961. A six-foot-six former University of Oklahoma basketball player, Schwall started the season with the Red Sox farm club in Seattle in the Pacific Coast League. Although he didn't appear in his first major league game until May 21, he pitched well enough to make the All-Star team. On August 7, Schwall had a record of 13-2 before missing two weeks with a kidney ailment. He finished the season at 15-7 with an ERA of 3.22 and won the American League Rookie of the Year Award over teammate Carl Yastrzemski. It was Schwall's last run of success in the majors, however. In 1962, he had a 9-15 record and was traded to the Pirates at the end of the season. Schwall's big-league career ended in 1967 with 49 wins and 48 losses.

**B**

# 17
## July

**O**n this date in 1956, Ted Williams hit his 400th career home run. When Williams crossed the plate after he hit the milestone homer, he showed his contempt for the Boston sportswriters (with whom he had an on-going adversarial relationship) by looking up at the press box and pursing his lips as if to spit, then sneered for an instant before disappearing into the dugout. Williams said later that he'd intended to spit, but held back because he was afraid he would hit teammate Mickey Vernon in the on-deck circle. Three nights later, Williams spit toward the press box after hitting a home run against the Tigers. On August 7, Williams dropped a fly ball in the outfield and was booed. After Williams made a leaping catch to end the inning, the crowd cheered. Enraged by the fickle nature of the fans, he spat toward the crowd behind first base, then repeated the act toward third base before entering the dugout. In the bottom of the inning, with the bases loaded, Williams spat twice more as he walked to the plate, once in the direction of the Yankee bench. After walking to force in the winning run for a 1-0 victory, Williams tossed his bat 40 feet into the air. The Red Sox responded by fining Williams $5,000.

**B**

**18**
July

**O**n this date in 1939, the Red Sox sold Pee Wee Reese to the Dodgers for four minor league players and $75,000. Reese was five days shy of his 21st birthday and was playing for the Red Sox farm club at Louisville in the American Association. Most considered Reese to be the best shortstop prospect in the minor leagues. Joe Cronin, Boston's starting shortstop as well as the manager, was 32 years old and believed he had five years left him in. Cronin told reporters that he didn't think it was fair to keep Reese waiting that long. In 1939, Cronin hit .308 and clubbed 19 homers. He stepped aside as the Red Sox starting shortstop in 1942 in favor of Johnny Pesky. Reese was the regular shortstop for the Dodgers from 1940 until 1956 and was elected to the Hall of Fame in 1984.

# 19
## July

**I**ndians shortstop Neal Ball pulled off an unassisted triple play on this date in 1909 during a 6-1 Red Sox loss in Cleveland. With Heinie Wagner on second base and Jake Stahl on first in the second inning, Amby McConnell hit a vicious liner to Ball. The infielder stepped on second to force out Wagner and tagged out Stahl, who was two strides from second. It was the first officially recognized unassisted triple play in baseball history. In the bottom of the second, Ball hit a home run, his first in the majors. He hit only four in 1,609 career at-bats.

# 20
## July

On this date in 1990, Red Sox reliever Rob Murphy tore up the clubhouse, smashing candy bowls with a baseball bat. He'd given up three runs in two-thirds of an inning during a 5-0 loss to the Royals in Kansas City. Later in the same series, he threw his glove into the outfield after being taken out of a game. Sox fans shuddered every time Murphy entered a game as he suffered through a horrible year in 1990, posting an 0-6 record and an ERA of 6.32 in 57 innings over 68 appearances. On May 7, he shaved in the middle of a three-inning relief stint against the Mariners in Seattle. Murphy came into the game in the seventh with the Red Sox holding a 5-2 lead, then gave up two runs in the eighth that narrowed the gap to one run. When he finally secured the last out in the eighth, Murphy stormed into the visitors' clubhouse, grabbed a razor and dry shaved his four-day beard. When he went to the mound for the ninth inning, he had a different look and got the last three outs to preserve a 5-4 victory. A superstitious sort, Murphy also refused to pitch unless he was wearing black underwear.

# 21
## July

**T**ed Williams created controversy on this date in 1940 during a conversation with Cleveland writer Harry Grayson. Williams talked about visiting his uncle, who was a fireman, at his firehouse in Yonkers. It was a quiet day at the firehouse, and everyone was lounging in the sun. "Hell you can live like this and retire with a pension," Williams told Grayson. "Here I am hitting .340 and everybody's all over me. Maybe I shoulda been a fireman." Williams further contended that his $12,500 salary was "chicken feed." Responding to Williams's regrets about not being a fireman, White Sox manager Jimmy Dykes supplied his club with bells, sirens and fire hats during a series against the Red Sox in Chicago, which began on July 23, and goaded the Red Sox slugger every time he came to bat.

**22**
July

**T**he question of the day.

Who was Chuck Koney?

Chuck Koney was a Red Sox minor leaguer who was playing for Louisville in the American Association when he lost his right leg after a water heater explosion at his home in Chicago on May 9, 1949. The blast of water and metal burned and nearly tore off his leg, necessitating amputation. Koney was recovering from another injury when he'd left the Louisville club and traveled to Chicago to see his wife and two-year-old son. Two days after the accident, Tom Yawkey gave Koney a five-year contract as a scout. Koney was employed by the Red Sox as a scout for more than 40 years before retiring.

# 23
## July

**O**n this date in 2002, Nomar Garciaparra hit three homers, two of them in one inning, and drove in eight runs to beat the Devil Rays 24-2 at Fenway Park. It was Garciparra's 29th birthday. Tampa Bay led 4-0 before the Sox exploded for 10 runs in the third inning. Garciaparra set a major league record for most homers in an inning with two, connecting off Tanyon Sturtze and Brandon Backe. In the fourth, Garciaparra clubbed a grand slam off Backe. The only other Red Sox players with two homers in an inning are Bill Regan in 1928, Ellis Burks in 1990 and David Ortiz in 2008. Garciaparra also tied a big-league mark for most home runs in consecutive games with five. The previous day, he homered twice during a 9-8 loss to the Yankees in New York. The only other Red Sox hitter with five homers in back-to-back games is Carl Yastrzemski in 1976.

**24**
**July**

**A**fter scoring a total of six runs in five road defeats from July 19 through July 23, the Red Sox tried a little voodoo to drive the evil spirits from their bats on this date in 1990. In a scene inspired by the hit movie *Major League*, Mike Greenwell, Wade Boggs and Tony Peña built an altar in the Milwaukee clubhouse. Above it they put a number 13 jersey with a rope tied around the neck and a stuffed rooster pinned to the tail. A Buddha statue, vigil candles and rubber spiders and snakes were placed on a table. The club's bats were then put around the table and left until game time. The Sox scored five runs, but lost 6-5 to the Brewers in 10 innings.

**B**

# 25
## July

**O**n this date in 1941, Lefty Grove won his 300th career game with a 10-6 victory over the Indians at Fenway Park. It was Grove's third attempt to collect number 300. The Red Sox trailed 4-0 after Grove allowed a run in the second inning and two in the third. The Sox tied the score 4-4, only to fall behind again 6-4 when Grove surrendered two runs in the seventh. Boston came back once more with two tallies in their half of the seventh on a Jim Tabor home run, then four more in the eighth. Jimmie Foxx broke a 6-6 tie with a two-run triple. Grove made six more starts but failed to win another game. His final big-league appearance came on September 28, the last day of the season, when he pitched one inning and gave up three runs and four hits against the Athletics in Philadelphia. Grove was released by the Red Sox at the end of the 1941 season, and after failing to hook up with another club, decided to retire. His .680 winning percentage is the best of any of the 23 pitchers who have won at least 300 games through 2008.

**B**

# 26
## July

**R**ed Sox players Gene Conley and Pumpsie Green participated in one of the most bizarre disappearances in the history of baseball on this date in 1962. It all began on a bus that took the club from Yankee Stadium to the Newark Airport. Leaving Yankee Stadium at 5:20 p.m., the air conditioning on the Sox' bus broke down in a massive traffic jam. It was hot, and Conley was getting irritable and had to use the men's room. There wasn't one on the bus, so he told manager Pinky Higgins that he was going to a washroom in a nearby garage. Green went with him. The traffic began to move, and the team bus took off without Conley and Green. Higgins wasn't sure the two players would get to Washington in time for the twinight double-header at 6 p.m. the next day. Instead of going to Washington, Conley and Green went to a bar, then to downtown Manhattan and checked into the Hotel Commodore. On the afternoon of July 27, Conley had an inspiration: He decided to go to Jerusalem. Green opted to rejoin the team in Washington. Conley called the Israeli Airlines to make a reservation for that evening. When he got to the airline ticket desk, he couldn't purchase a ticket because he didn't have a passport. Conley went back to the hotel for a day, where he was met by his wife and children. He returned to the Red Sox on July 30.

# 27
## July

**O**n this date in 1946, Red Sox first baseman Rudy York drove in 10 runs on a pair of grand slams, leading the Red Sox to a 13-6 win over the Browns in St. Louis. In the first inning, York doubled in two runs off Bob Muncrief after Ted Williams drew an intentional walk. In the second, Williams walked to load the bases, and York followed with a homer off Tex Shirley. In the fifth, Williams was again given an intentional walk to load the bases, and facing Shirley again, York hit his second grand slam of the game. Rudy also came to bat in the seventh and ninth innings. He struck out with one runner on base and hit into a double play with two on.

# 28
## July

On this date in 1991, pitcher Jeff Gray suffered a stroke before a 5-2 loss to the White Sox at Fenway Park. Gray was in the locker room preparing to go out on the field and talking to teammates Jeff Reardon and Joe Hesketh when he slumped to the floor. Gray's speech was slurred, and his right side was paralyzed. After an examination, it was determined that he'd suffered a slight stroke caused by an enlarged blood vessel in his brain. Only 28 when he was stricken, Gray never played another major league game.

B

# 29
## July

**O**n this date in 1988, the Red Sox traded prospects Curt Schilling and Brady Anderson for Mike Boddicker. Anderson opened the 1988 season as the Sox' starting center fielder but was sent to Pawtucket in May. Schilling was at Class AA New Britain and had yet to appear in a big-league game. In the short term, this was an excellent trade. If the Sox hadn't completed the swap, it's unlikely the club would have reached the postseason in either 1988 and 1990. Neither Anderson nor Schilling were ready for the majors by that time, and Boddicker provided a necessary veteran presence to the pitching staff. In the long haul, the deal was a disaster. It took awhile for Anderson to develop into a valuable major leaguer, but from 1992 through 1999, he was among the best outfielders in the American League. In 1996, Anderson hit 50 homers for the Orioles. Schilling, too, spent come difficult years early in the majors. Heading into the 1992 season, he had a career record of 4-11 with the Phillies and Astros. From 1992 through 2003, Schilling was 159-106 for the Phillies and Diamondbacks and returned to the Red Sox organization in a trade in November 2003. He became a New England folk hero with a 21-6 record during the regular season in 2004 and before recording three postseason wins while battling a serious ankle injury.

# 30
## July

**O**n this date in 1991, Carlos Quintana tied an American League record by driving in six runs in an inning during an 11-6 win over the Rangers at Fenway Park. In the third inning, Quintana hit a grand slam off Oil Can Boyd and a two-run double against Wayne Rosenthal. The Sox scored 10 runs in the inning to take an 11-2 lead. The win ended the Sox' nine-game losing streak at Fenway, the club's longest since 1927. Quintana is one of three Red Sox with six runs batted in in an inning. The other two are Tom McBride on August 4, 1945, and David Ortiz on August 12, 2008. Quintana missed the entire 1992 season after being in an auto accident in which he broke his arm. The accident occurred in his native Venezuela while Quintana was rushing his two brothers to the hospital after they had been shot at a party. He returned to the Sox in 1993, but was still suffering from the effects of the accident and lost his job as a starting first baseman to Mo Vaughn.

# 31
## July

On this date in 1991, Jack Clark hit three home runs, the last one a walk-off blast in the 14th off Steve Chiltren, to beat the Athletics 11-10 at Fenway Park. Earlier, Clark hit a grand slam in the third against Dave Stewart and a solo shot facing Gene Nelson in the eighth. The Sox trailed 10-6 before scoring three runs in the eighth and one in the ninth. The Red Sox signed Clark for three years at $8.5 million in December 1990, but he gave the club only one productive season before slumping in 1992, hitting only .210 with five homers. He ended up as a villain in Boston, booed by the fans and ripped by the media. Just after the All-Star break in 1992, he declared bankruptcy because he was $6.7 million in debt. Clark had sponsored a drag racing enterprise, which lost $1 million a year; built a multi-million-dollar mansion he was forced to sell; operated a restaurant that was losing money; and owned 18 automobiles. Clark was released at the end of the 1992 season, ending his 18-year career.

B

# August

# B

# 01
## August

On this date in 1973, the Red Sox defeated the Yankees 3-2 at Fenway Park in a contest highlighted by a brawl between Carlton Fisk and Thurman Munson. In the ninth inning, Yankee batter Gene Michael attempted a suicide squeeze bunt with Munson on third. Michael missed but tried to get in Fisk's way as he stepped forward to tag Munson coming down the line. Fisk brushed Michael aside with one swipe of his arm, and Munson barreled into Fisk. Fisk held onto the ball for the out, with Munson landing on top of him. Fisk flipped Munson, who came up swinging. Fisticuffs followed with Michael leaping over Munson to get in a few swings at Fisk, and the Red Sox catcher managed to pin Michael's neck to the ground. Yankee manager Ralph Houk had to crawl through a pile to pull Fisk's elbow off Michael's throat and allow him to breathe. Both Fisk and Munson were ejected, but Michael was allowed to stay in the game, prompting a long argument from Sox manager Eddie Kasko. Fisk emerged with a scratch on his face and a bruised eye. Bob Montgomery, Fisk's replacement, started the game-winning rally with a single.

# 02
## August

**O**n this date in 1904, four Red Sox put out a fire after a 4-1 win over the Indians in Cleveland. Just after arriving at the hotel, Hobe Ferris, Freddie Parent, Bill Dinneen and Norwood Gibson noticed flames bursting from a room and several panic-stricken employees running about the fifth floor. The four dashed out of the elevator, and after the fire had spread from one room to another, managed to put out the blaze using a fire hose without calling the fire department. Ferris was the Red Sox starting second baseman from 1901 through 1907 and was involved in a cowardly incident two years after helping put out the fire. He and teammate Jack Hayden engaged in a vicious flight on the field during an 11-3 loss to the Yankees in New York on September 11, 1906. Ferris accused Hayden of loafing, and Hayden retaliated by punching Ferris. As Hayden was about to sit down on the bench, Ferris kicked him in the mouth. His spikes sliced open Hayden's face in several places. Ferris was suspended by the Red Sox for the remainder of the season. Hayden missed the rest of the year nursing the injuries inflicted by Ferris and never played another game for the club.

# 03
## August

**T**he question of the day.
What team took batting practice in a Boston hotel lobby?
The California Angels took batting practice in the lobby of the Sheraton Hotel in Boston on May 24, 1975, before losing to Bill Lee and the Red Sox 6-0 at Fenway Park in a contest nationally televised on NBC. A couple of days earlier, Lee had told reporters that the weak-hitting Angels "could take batting practice in a hotel lobby without breaking a chandelier." Angels manager Dick Williams decided to go along with the gag. He told his players to report to the lobby instead of the ballpark at noon. With plastic bats and Nerf balls, Williams pitched to Winston Llenas before hotel security officers ordered an end to the hijinks. Lee pitched the complete game shutout, allowing just four hits.

# 04
## August

**O**n this date in 1945, the Red Sox scored 12 runs in the fourth inning to break a 2-2 tie and went on to defeat the Senators 15-4 in Washington. The game took place two weeks prior to Japan's surrender, ending the Second World War. Outfielder Tom McBride tied an American league record by driving in six runs in the inning. He cleared the bases twice with a double and a triple. Bert Shepard pitched the final 5⅓ innings for the Senators, allowing one run and three hits. Shepard pitched on a wooden leg after losing the lower part of his right leg in aerial combat over Germany. It was his only major league appearance.

# 05
## August

**O**n this date in 1935, the Red Sox lost a controversial 10-2 decision to the Yankees at Fenway Park that was called after five innings due to rain. With rain falling and the Yankees leading 8-2 in the top of the fifth, the Red Sox made no attempt to retire the opposition in the hopes the game would be called before the legal five innings. The Yankees, on the other hand, tried to make outs deliberately to speed the game to a conclusion. In one instance, Red Sox third baseman Billy Werber threw wildly on a grounder by George Selkirk, who loped around the bases for several minutes until somebody tagged him out. On another play, Myril Hoag of the Yankees jogged in from third base and crossed the plate with a steal of home without anyone from the Sox making a play on him. The pitcher on Hoag's "steal" on home was Stew Bowers, making his major league debut. Red Sox manager Joe Cronin and Yankee skipper Joe McCarthy were both fined $100 by the American League for their part in the farce

**06**
**August**

**T**he question of the day.
Who was Bill Lee?
During his 10 seasons with
the Red Sox from 1969 through 1978,
Bill Lee was outrageous, irreverent and
fascinating. He earned the nickname
"Space Man" because of his unusual but
entertaining and often hilarious ideas. For
instance, Lee said that the Red Sox should
hire beautiful women as first- and third-base
coaches. "That way, the players would pay attention," Lee said, "and
would never miss a sign." He ate health food, practiced yoga and
claimed that the use of marijuana made him impervious to bus
fumes while jogging to Fenway Park. Lee defended Maoist China,
population control, Greenpeace and school busing in Boston. His
acid tongue and frequent criticism of team managers divided the
Red Sox Nation into pro-Lee and anti-Lee factions. Few were am-
bivalent. He became a cult hero to young fans and unnerved the
baseball establishment with his personal explorations into Eastern
religions, pacifism, and drugs and rock 'n' roll. Despite his flaky,
paradoxical and iconoclastic persona, Lee was an avowed purist
when it came to baseball, criticizing the designated hitter and
AstroTurf. One of the most competitive players in the game, Lee
had no qualms about throwing at hitters or getting into brawls.

# 07
## August

**T**he question of the day.

Who was Dick Radatz?

For three seasons, Dick Radatz was the most dominating relief pitcher in baseball. He created a sensation as a 25-year-old rookie in 1962 with a 9-5 record, a league-leading 24 saves, a 2.24 earned run average, and 144 strikeouts in 62 games and 124⅔ innings. At six-foot-five and 235 pounds, Radatz possessed a devastating fastball, earning him the nickname "The Monster." In 1963, he pitched 33 consecutive innings of scoreless relief, in which he struck out 53 batters. Overall, Radatz had a 15-6 record and 25 saves. His ERA was 1.97, and he struck out 162 batters in 132⅓ innings over 66 games. In the All-Star Game, he struck out five batters in two innings. Radatz had his third sensational year in a row in 1964, posting a 16-9 record, 29 saves and a 2.29 ERA. Radatz struck out 181 batters (the all-time record for a reliever in a season) over 157 innings in 79 games. From 1962 through 1964, Radatz made 207 relief appearances, hurled 414 innings, struck out 487 batters and had an ERA of 2.17. He had a 40-20 record and 78 saves on three Red Sox teams with losing records. The heavy workload took a toll, however, and Radatz was never again effective after 1964. Over the remainder of his career, which ended in 1969, Radatz had an ERA of 4.54.

**08**
**August**

**O**n this date in 1976, rookie pitcher Rick Jones missed a flight to Anaheim. The following morning, Jones was spotted by one club official walking around Kenmore Square, but when he arrived in Anaheim later that night, Jones told manager Don Zimmer that he had gone to Florida to visit his sick father. At the time, Jones was 21 and showed some promise with a 4-1 record and a 2.84 ERA, but because of the missed flight, several missed curfews and his general immaturity, the Sox sent him back to Pawtucket. He came back to the club in September, pitched ineffectively and went to the Mariners in the expansion draft. Jones's big-league career ended in 1978 when he was only 23. Three of his high school buddies were members of the rock band Lynyrd Skynyrd, named after Leonard Skinner, their football coach at Forrest High School in Jacksonville, Florida, who had suspended Jones and the band members from the athletic program because they refused to cut their hair.

**B**

# 09
## August

**I**n one of the weirdest games in Boston baseball history, the Red Sox scored all of their runs in the final three innings to defeat the Athletics 16-4 in Philadelphia on this date in 1938. The Sox scored seven runs in the seventh inning, three in the eighth and six in the ninth. Not only were the Red Sox held scoreless through the first six innings, but the club had nary a base runner as Athletics starter Nelson Potter retired the first 18 batters to face him. But Potter came apart at the seams in the seventh. Four of the runs scored on a grand slam by Jim Tabor. It was the first homer of his career, and it came seven days after his big-league debut. Tabor was a third baseman for the Red Sox from 1938 through 1944. In 1939, Tabor was suspended for three days by manager Joe Cronin "for the good of the team and to discipline him a little." Cronin refused to go into details, merely saying that Tabor "hasn't been acting too well lately." It was no secret that Tabor was a hard drinker, so there is little doubt that alcohol abuse led to the suspension. He also didn't hesitate to speak his mind. Tabor died of a heart attack in 1953 when he was only 36.

**10**
**August**

**T**he question of the day.
Who is the only player in Red Sox history to hit four home runs in a double-header?

On July 4, 1939, Jim Tabor staged a holiday hit parade by swatting four home runs, including two grand slams, during a double-header against the Athletics in Philadelphia. He scored seven runs and had 11 runs batted in. The Red Sox won 17-7 and 18-12 as the two teams combined for 54 runs and 65 hits. In the first game, Tabor had a single, a double and a homer in five at-bats. He drove in two runs and scored twice. In the second tilt, Tabor hit three home runs in four at-bats, scored five runs and drove in nine in one of the greatest single-game explosions in Red Sox history. Two of the three homers were grand slams, one in the third inning against George Caster and another off Chubby Dean in the sixth. Tabor was the first player in Red Sox history to hit three homers in a game. The second was Ted Williams in 1946. Despite the four home runs, Tabor's accomplishment was overshadowed on the nation's sports pages the following day by Lou Gehrig Day at Yankee Stadium. Weeks after being diagnosed with ALS, Gehrig stepped to the microphone and told fans he considered himself "the luckiest man on the face of the earth."

**B**

# 11
## August

**H**appy Birthday Bill Monbouquette.

A pitcher with the Red Sox from 1958 through 1965, Bill Monbouquette was born on this date in 1936. Although later in his career he was saddled with hurling for a string of losing teams, Monbouquette had some big moments with the Sox, including being named to three All-Star teams. On May 12, 1961, he struck out 17 batters during a 2-1 win over the Senators in Washington. The 17 strikeouts stood as the club record until Roger Clemens fanned 20 in 1986. Monbouquette no-hit the White Sox on August 1, 1962, for a 1-0 win at Comiskey Park. It was the second Red Sox no-hitter in five weeks, following the one by Earl Wilson on July 26. The lone Chicago base runner was Al Smith, who walked on a 3-2 pitch with two outs in the second inning. Monbouquette retired the next 22 batters in a row. In the ninth inning, he struck out Sherm Lollar for the first out, retired Nellie Fox on a grounder to third baseman Frank Malzone and fanned Luis Aparicio. Monbouquette struck out seven batters. Lu Clinton drove in Jim Pagliaroni off Early Wynn in the eighth inning for the game's only run. In his four previous starts prior to his no-hitter, Monbouquette allowed 17 runs in 10⅔ innings. In 1963, on a club that was 76-85, he posted a record of 20-10.

**B**

# 12 August

**T**he question of the day.
Who was Mel Parnell? From 1948 through 1953, Mel Parnell was one of the top pitchers in baseball, posting a record of 109-56 over that stretch, including marks of 25-7 in 1949 and 21-8 in 1953. No Red Sox pitcher since Parnell has a season of 25 or more wins since he accomplished the feat. After 1953, he experienced a sharp downturn, however, and was 12-16 over three seasons before his career ended in 1956. He did have one moment of glory during his final season, however, with a no-hitter on July 14 in defeating the White Sox 4-0 before 14,542 at Fenway Park. It was the first Red Sox no-hitter since 1923. In the ninth inning, Parnell walked Sammy Esposito on a 3-2 pitch. Luis Aparicio followed with a grounder up the middle, which second baseman Billy Goodman stopped with a diving stab and flipped to shortstop Don Buddin for the force. Had there been no runner on first, Aparicio likely would have beat out the ball for a single. Bubba Phillips also hit into a force from third baseman Billy Klaus to Goodman for the second out. The game ended when Walt Dropo tapped the ball to the right of the mound, where Parnell fielded it and raced all the way to first for the unassisted out. Parnell walked two and struck out four.

# 13
## August

On this date in 1908, a crowd of 20,000 attended Cy Young Day at Huntington Grounds as the Red Sox defeated a team of All-Stars from the other seven American League teams 3-2 in 11 innings. The Red Sox played in costumes, which included an admiral, a clown and a cowboy. Manager Deacon McGuire was dressed as Uncle Sam, while Young appeared as a farmer. Political correctness definitely wasn't in vogue in 1908, as others were dressed as a "Chinaman," a "country dude," a "Swedish comedian," and an "Irish comedian," while another was in blackface in the style of the minstrel shows of the period. Young received cash gifts of close to $7,500 plus three silver loving cups, traveling bags and two large floral pieces.

# 14
## August

The question of the day.
Who did the Red Sox trade for Larry Andersen?

In the second-worse transaction in club history, behind only the sale of Babe Ruth, the Red Sox sent Jeff Bagwell to the Astros for Larry Andersen on August 31, 1990. Andersen pitched only a month for the Sox before leaving as a free agent. Meanwhile, Bagwell reached the majors with the Astros in 1991 and became a star, winning the Rookie of the Year Award with a .294 average and 15 homers. Within two years, Bagwell was one of the best players in baseball and maintained the position for more than a decade. At the time of the trade, the Red Sox were concerned with Bagwell's potential as a power hitter, and the only positions he could play adequately were first and third. In 1990, the club had the best third baseman in baseball in Wade Boggs, and Mo Vaughn put together a tremendous season as a first baseman that year at Class AAA Pawtucket. The Sox also believed that Scott Cooper, who played third at Pawtucket in 1990, was going to be a star. So Bagwell seemed expendable, but that was a huge miscalculation. He finished his career in 2005 with 449 home runs and a .297 batting average. Those numbers would likely have been much higher had Bagwell played at cozy Fenway Park instead of the cavernous Astrodome.

# 15
## August

**O**n this date in 1941, the Red Sox won a forfeit in Washington because the Senators failed to cover the infield during a rainstorm. The game was stopped by a rain delay in the eighth inning with the Senators leading 6-3. For some reason, the grounds crew didn't cover the infield, and the contest was called after 40 minutes because the umpires deemed the field to be unplayable. Manager Joe Cronin protested to American League president Will Harridge that the contest would have resumed if the tarp had been spread on the infield. Harridge agreed and forfeited the game to Boston.

**B**

**16 August**

**O**n this date in 1936, Red Sox pitcher Wes Ferrell walked off the mound without warning during a four-run Washington eighth inning that put the Senators ahead 7-3 at Fenway Park. Since Cronin didn't have a pitcher warming up, he was forced to use Jack Russell, cold, as a reliever. The Red Sox went on to lose 7-6. In his next start five days later, Ferrell again stormed off the mound in the middle of a game. It happened in the sixth inning of a 4-1 loss to the Yankees in New York after shortstop Eric McNair made a critical error. Cronin responded to the unauthorized departure by fining Ferrell $1,000 and handing him an indefinite suspension. Ferrell threatened to beat Cronin to a pulp. "If he wants to slug me," said Cronin, "I'll be passing through the lobby at six o'clock on my way to dinner." Ferrell never showed. On August 26, Ferrell returned from his "indefinite suspension" without missing a start and pitched a shutout to defeat the Tigers 7-0 at Fenway Park.

# 17
## August

**O**n this date in 1904, Red Sox pitcher Jesse Tannehill pitched a no-hitter to defeat the White Sox 6-0 in Chicago. He walked one batter in the first inning before retiring 25 batters in a row while striking out four. With one out in the ninth, shortstop Freddie Parent preserved the no-hitter with a fine play on a ground ball to beat Danny Green at first base by a split second. The final out was recorded on a bouncer off the bat of Fielder Jones to second baseman Hobe Ferris. Jesse's younger brother Lee started at third base for the White Sox and was 0-for-3.

**B**

**18**
**August**

**I**n one of the worst tragedies in baseball history, Tony Conigliaro was beaned by Jack Hamilton on this date in 1967. Conigliaro was hit in the face, which knocked him unconscious, caused a severe hemorrhage of his nose, broke his cheekbone and sent bone fragments into his left eye. The day after the injury, doctors predicted Conigliaro would be playing again in two weeks. But within days it became apparent that the damage caused by the beaning was much more serious when his eyesight failed to return to normal. Conigliaro missed the rest of the 1967 season and all of 1968. He returned in 1969 but had problems with his eyesight for the remainder of his career, which ended in July 1971 with the exception of a brief comeback in 1975. How good would Conigliaro have been if he hadn't been hurt? On July 23, 1967, he became the second-youngest player in baseball history to hit 100 career homers at 22 years and 197 days. The youngest was future Hall of Famer Mel Ott, who accomplished the feat in 22 years and 132 days.

# 19
## August

**O**n this date in 1972, Luis Tiant pitched a two-hitter to defeat the White Sox 3-0 in Chicago. It was Tiant's first shutout since April 26, 1970, when he pitched for the Twins. Over the next 32 days, he would pitch five more shutouts. On August 25, Luis pitched his second straight shutout, defeating the Rangers 4-0 in Boston. On August 29, Tiant hurled his third consecutive shutout, downing the White Sox 3-0 at Fenway Park. On September 4, Tiant supplied his fourth shutout in a row with a 2-0 win over the Brewers in Milwaukee. Tiant defeated the Indians 10-0 at Fenway on September 16. And on September 20, Luis beat the Orioles 4-0 in Boston. Altogether, Tiant pitched six shutouts over a span of eight starts from August 19 through September 20, 1972, in which he allowed five runs in 68⅓ innings, an ERA of 0.66.

# 20
## August

**T**he question of the day. Who is the only player to play for both the Celtics and the Red Sox?

Gene Conley is the only athlete to play for both the Red Sox and Celtics. Standing six-foot-eight, Conley was a star in both baseball and basketball at Washington State University. He made his major league debut as a pitcher with the Boston Braves in April 1952. That fall, he also played for the Celtics. Conley gave up professional basketball to concentrate on baseball and made the All-Star team with the Braves in both 1954 and 1955 after the club moved to Milwaukee. In 1957, Conley played in the World Series for the Braves, who beat the Yankees in seven games. After an 0-6 season with Milwaukee in 1958, Conley returned to the Celtics as a back-up center to Bill Russell during the 1958–59 campaign. It was the first of three consecutive seasons in which he played for the Celts, each of which resulted in an NBA championship. He continued his basketball career with the New York Knicks in 1962–63 and 1963–64. From April 1958 through March 1964, Conley played both baseball and basketball year-round without a break. He played for the Phillies in 1959 and 1960 and for the Red Sox from 1961 through 1963. His best season for the Sox was 1962 when he was 15-14 in 241⅔ innings.

B

# 21
## August

**O**n this date in 1986, the Red Sox smashed the Indians 24-5 in Cleveland. The Sox scored 12 runs in the sixth inning, 11 of them with two out on four singles, a double, a home run and five walks, to take an 18-1 lead. Boston batters collected 24 hits. The first six runs were given up by Cleveland starter Greg Swindell, who was making his major league debut. In only his third game with the Red Sox, following a trade with the Mariners, shortstop Spike Owen tied a modern major league record by scoring six runs after reaching base on a homer, three singles and two walks. Owen is one of only three players in AL history to score six runs in a game. Johnny Pesky, also a shortstop for the Red Sox, scored six times on May 8, 1946. The Royals' Joe Randa did it in 2004. Pesky's six-run game came during a 14-10 victory over the White Sox at Fenway Park. Owen played three seasons with the Red Sox and batted only .244 with eight homers in 263 games. Spike was not a nickname, but Owen's real first name. His full name was Spike Dee Owen.

**22**
**August**

**O**n this date in 1975, Luis Tiant was reunited with his parents. He hadn't seen his father since 1961 or his mother since 1968 because both were trapped in Cuba, unable leave. Nor was Tiant allowed to visit his native country. Fidel Castro permitted Tiant's parents to leave Cuba for a visit to the United States after responding to a request from Massachusetts Senator Edward Brooke. That winter, both of Tiant's parents died within three months of each other.

# 23
## August

**B**ehind the pitching of Tex Hughson and Joe Dobson, the Red Sox shut out the Athletics in both ends of a twin bill in Philadelphia on this date in 1942 by scores of 2-0 and 7-0. In the second game, fans in the left-field stands at Shibe Park showered Ted Williams with garbage. Police were called in to quell the disturbance. For his own protection, Williams left the game in the ninth inning. The contests were played eight months after the attack on Pearl Harbor, and the gate receipts were donated to the Army-Navy Relief Fund. The crowd of 26,014 witnessed a display of America's military might between games, staged by mechanized Troop A of the United States cavalry stationed in Philadelphia. It included a display of armored scout cars, two-way radios, jeeps and motorcycles.

**24**
**August**

**O**n this date in 1940, Ted Williams pitched two innings during a 10-1 loss to the Tigers in the first game of a double-header at Fenway Park. Williams allowed a run and three hits and struck out one. This was the only game that Williams pitched during his big-league career. His catcher was Joe Glenn, who also caught the last game that Babe Ruth pitched while with the Yankees in 1933. Glenn played only 22 games in a Boston uniform, in which he hit .128.

**B**

# 25

## August

**A** 1-0 win over the Twins at Metropolitan Stadium in Bloomington, Minnesota, was interrupted for 43 minutes on this date in 1970 because of a bomb scare. An anonymous caller informed police that the bomb would explode at 9:30 p.m. At 9:15 p.m., during the fourth inning, the crowd of 17,697 was told to file calmly out of the ballpark. After a search found nothing, play resumed at 9:58 p.m. The lone run of the contest scored in the eighth inning on a home run by Tony Conigliaro. On September 1, bomb threats were phoned in to Fenway Park. Unlike in Minnesota a week earlier, the game wasn't stopped, and only a portion of the ballpark was evacuated. The caller stated that the bomb was planted in the bleachers, and fans in that section were ordered to move into the right-field stands to allow the Boston bomb squad to conduct a search, which fortunately, found no explosive devices.

# 26
## August

On this date in 1957, the Red Sox hit four home runs in an inning for the second time during the season, creating a club record. The home runs came in the seventh inning of a 16-0 trouncing of the Athletics in Kansas City in the process of piling up 10 runs. Frank Malzone, Norm Zauchin, Ted Lepcio and Jimmy Piersall accounted for the quartet of homers. The other times it happened were on September 24, 1940 (Ted Williams, Jimmy Foxx, Joe Cronin and Jim Tabor), May 22, 1957 (Gene Mauch, Williams, Dick Gernert and Malzone), July 4, 1977 (Fred Lynn, Jim Rice, Carl Yastrzemski and George Scott), May 31, 1980 (Dave Stapleton, Tony Perez, Carlton Fisk and Butch Hobson), July 18, 1998 (Donnie Sadler, Darren Lewis, Nomar Garciaparra and Mo Vaughn), July 3, 2000 (Carl Everett, Troy O'Leary, Jason Varitek and Morgan Burkhart), July 23, 2002 (two by Garciaparra and one each by Johnny Damon and Manny Ramirez) and April 22, 2007 (Ramirez, J. D. Drew, Mike Lowell and Varitek). The four in the 2007 game were consecutive.

# 27
## August

**T**he question of the day.

How did a base-running mishap help cost the Red Sox the AL East pennant in 1972?

The Red Sox and Tigers ended the 1972 season with a pennant-showdown series in Detroit on October 1, 2 and 3. Whichever team won two of three would claim the division title. The Tigers took the first two games 4-1 and 3-1 to move on to the postseason. A base-running mishap proved costly in the first game. With the score 1-0 Tigers in the Boston half of the third inning, the Sox had Tommy Harper on third base and Luis Aparicio on first. When Carl Yastrzemski hit a drive off the top of the center-field wall, Harper crossed the plate with the tying run. Aparicio was headed for the go-ahead tally when he stumbled as he neared third, regained his balance, and fell down awkwardly in foul territory. Yastrzemski had designs on a triple and, running head down, didn't see Aparicio fall. Yaz arrived at third only to see Aparicio on the bag. Aparicio tried to head for home, but slipped and fell again on the wet grass and had to scramble back to third again. In the process, he cut his knee with his own spikes. Yaz tried to retreat to second and was tagged out.

**B**

# 28
## August

On this date in 1956, a bone-headed play by catcher Sammy White and his Boston teammates contributed to a 6-3 loss to the Tigers at Fenway Park. With the Tigers leading 4-0 in the sixth inning and Detroit's Bill Tuttle on second base, Red Wilson poked a grounder through the middle of the infield. Red Sox shortstop Milt Bolling fielded the ball behind second base and was surprised to see Tuttle heading for the plate. Bolling threw home, and umpire Frank Umont ruled that Tuttle was safe. White vehemently protested the decision and threw the ball into center field. While the Red Sox continued to argue, they failed to notice Wilson was running around the bases. As he reached home, Wilson had to brush against Umont, who was sweeping off the plate. Since the Red Sox failed to call time, the umpires had no choice but to award the Tigers a run.

# 29
## August

**O**n this date in 2000, Pedro Martinez struck out 13 batters and came within three outs of a no-hitter, and Carl Everett drove in six runs by hitting home runs from both sides of the plate during a brawl-filled 8-0 win over the Devil Rays in St. Petersburg. After hitting leadoff man Gerald Williams in the first inning on just the fourth pitch of the night, Martinez retired 24 batters in a row before John Flaherty hit a lead-off single to right-center on a 2-2 pitch in the ninth. Martinez then retired the next three batters to finish with a one-hitter. Umpires ejected eight Devil Rays, including five players, in the first seven innings of the game, which featured five confrontations. Tampa Bay manager Larry Rothschild and Williams were ejected in the first inning. Williams charged the mound after Martinez hit him and set off a bench-clearing brawl. The game was delayed 12 minutes. Dugouts emptied four times during the evening. Two Devil Rays coaches, serving as acting managers, were ejected after pitchers threw at Red Sox hitters in the third and seventh innings.

# 30 August

**O**n this date in 1960, Pete Runnels tied a major league record with nine hits in a double-header against the Tigers at Fenway Park. In the first game, Runnels collected six hits in seven at-bats. His sixth hit was a walk-off double in the 15th inning that gave the Red Sox a 5-4 victory. In the second tilt, Runnels was 3-for-4 during a 3-2 Boston win. He is one of four Red Sox players with a six-hit game. Jimmy Piersall picked up six hits, including a double, in six at-bats during an 11-2 win over the Browns in St. Louis on June 10, 1953. Piersall is the only Boston player to accomplish the feat in a nine-inning game. Jerry Remy had six singles in 10 at-bats during a 20-inning, 8-7 loss to the Mariners at Fenway Park that took two days to complete. It started on September 3, 1981, and was suspended at the end of the 19th inning with the score 7-7 because of the American League 1:00 a.m. curfew. The Sox trailed 7-3 before scoring a run in the eighth inning and three in the ninth. The game was tied on a two-run single by Joe Rudi and another run-scoring single from Rich Gedman. When the game resumed the following evening, Seattle scored in the 20th for the victory. It is the longest game in Fenway history.

# 31
## August

**O**n this date in 1918, the Red Sox clinched the American League pennant with a 6-1 victory over the Athletics at Fenway Park. The 1918 regular season ended on September 2 because of World War I. On August 1, baseball announced that the season would close early following an order from the federal government that all players of draft age either enlist or find war-related jobs such as working in a shipyard or a munitions factory. The World Series was scheduled to begin on September 4, although rain pushed back the opening one day. It is the earliest date ever for a Fall Classic in history. The Red Sox played the Chicago Cubs and won in six games. Ironically, if the Series had been played during its normal period in early October, it might have been canceled or postponed by a flu epidemic. From late September through November, a virulent form of influenza struck the nation. Public gatherings in many cities, including Boston and Chicago, were banned by health officials. Estimates are that 20 to 25 percent of the nation's population was struck by the flu. The epidemic caused 400,000 to 500,000 deaths in the United States and 20 million worldwide.

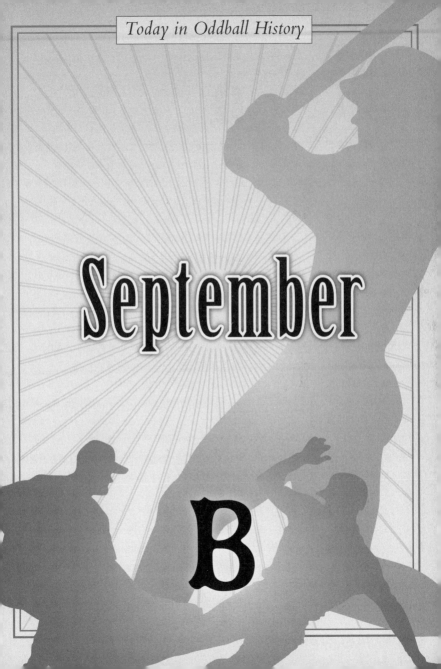

# September

B

# 01
## September

On this date in 2007, Clay Buchholz pitched a no-hitter in only his second major league start, defeating the Orioles 10-0 at Fenway Park. He became the first Red Sox rookie with a no-hitter: he threw 115 pitches, struck out nine, walked three, and hit one. General manager Theo Epstein and manager Terry Francona spoke on the phone during the seventh and eighth innings about Buchholz's pitch count. Epstein said after the game that there was no way that Buchholz would have been allowed to exceed 120 pitches. He became the third pitcher in major league history to pitch a no-hitter in two starts or less. Bobo Holloman did it for the Browns in his first start on May 6, 1953, and Wilson Alvarez of the White Sox in his second on August 11, 1991. In the ninth inning, Buchholz struck out Brian Roberts swinging, Corey Patterson on a line out to Coco Crisp in center field, and Nick Markakis on a strikeout looking.

**02**
**September**

On this date in 1996, Mike Green-well drove in all nine of the Red Sox runs in a ten-inning, 9-8 win over the Mariners in Seattle. Greenwell set a major league record while driving in all of a team's runs in a game. The previous record was eight by George Kelly of the Giants in 1924 and Bob John-son of the Athletics in 1938. The Red Sox were behind 5-0 when Greenwell hit a two-run homer off Bob Wolcott in the fifth inning. Greenwell put the Sox ahead with a grand slam in the sixth facing Bobby Ayala. The Mariners took an 8-6 lead with three runs in the seventh, however. Greenwell tied it 8-8 with a two-run double in the eighth against Norm Charlton. He also drove in the winning run in the 10th inning with a single off Rafael Carmona and accounted for four of the Red Sox' seven hits. Over the remainder of Greenwell's major league career, which ended at the close of the 1996 season, he drove in only 10 more runs. Greenwell played all 12 of his big-league seasons with the Red Sox and was the runner-up to Jose Canseco in the MVP voting in 1988. In an interview in 2008, Greenwell said he that believes the award is rightfully his since Canseco has admitted to steroid use.

# 03
## September

**A**fter the Red Sox beat the Yankees 12-11 in the first game of a double-header at Fenway Park, the two clubs played "stall ball" during a bizarre second game on this date in 1939. The Yankees scored two runs in the top of the eighth inning to take a 7-5 lead. The Sunday curfew of 6:30 p.m. was fast approaching. If the Red Sox didn't get to bat in the bottom of the eighth, the entire inning would be canceled and the score would revert back to 5-5. The Yankees were trying to make outs while the Red Sox were attempting to extend the game as long as possible. Boston pitcher Eldon Auker tried to issue an intentional walk to Babe Dahlgren, but the batter swung and missed at three pitches several feet wide of the plate and struck out. Both George Selkirk and Joe Gordon sauntered around the bases until they were tagged out. Many fans began to litter the field with bottles, straw hats, newspapers and garbage. Finally, the umpire declared the field unplayable and forfeited the game to the Yankees. The Red Sox protested the decision to AL president Will Harridge, who ordered that the game should go into the books as a 5-5 tie with a make-up scheduled for September 26. The rescheduled game was rained out, however, and never played.

B

**04**
**September**

**H**appy Birthday, Ken Harrelson.
A cult hero while playing for the Red Sox from 1967 through 1969, Ken Harrelson was born on this date in 1941. He signed a free-agent contract with the Sox on August 28, 1967, following his release by the Athletics, which was prompted by calling A's owner Charlie Finley a "menace to baseball." Harrelson was a productive front-line player, and the release made him a free agent. Teams lined up for his services. With Tony Conigliaro out for the season, the Red Sox needed a right fielder, and Harrelson fit the bill. The Red Sox won the bidding war by offering Harrelson a bonus of $75,000 at a time when only a small handful of superstars earned as much as $100,000 a season. Harrelson became an immensely popular figure in Boston with a great offensive season in 1968, an eccentric personality, Southern charm, long hair (one of the first athletes to wear long hair) and wildly colored "mod" outfits. Harrelson was a particular favorite of young fans in a city full of college students at the height of the antiestablishment rebellion against authority. Fitting right in with the changing times of the "psychedelic sixties," Harrelson drove to the ballpark in a lavender dune buggy with flowers on the roof. He even had a one-hour variety show on WHDH-TV entitled "The Hawk."

**B**

# 05
## September

**O**n this date in 1927, the Red Sox earned a sensational 12-11 victory in 18 innings in the first game of a double-header against the vaunted Yankees before a crowd of 34,385 at Fenway Park. About 15,000 stormed the gates of the ballpark after ticket sales stopped. The game started 20 minutes late because of the difficulty of getting the crowd under control. Hundreds swarmed all over the field, and patrolmen and mounted police were called in to clear the diamond. The Red Sox led the game 8-6 in the ninth when Earle Combs of the Yankees hit a two-out, two-run double to tie the score. After the Yankees took an 11-8 lead in the 17th inning, the Red Sox countered with three in their half. The tying run scored on a pinch-hit double by third-string catcher Billy Moore, who would have only two more doubles and four more RBIs during his major league career. The winning run came from doubles by Buddy Myer and Ira Flagstead off Waite Hoyt. Red Ruffing pitched 15 innings for the Red Sox, and Hal Wiltse hurled the final three. Wiltse also started the second game, which was called after five innings by darkness with the Yankees leading 5-0.

# 06
## September

**I**n one of the most storied pitching matchups in baseball history, Smoky Joe Wood of the Red Sox bested Walter Johnson and the Senators 1-0 on this date in 1912 before 30,000 on a Friday afternoon at Fenway Park. Earlier in the season, Johnson had won 16 consecutive games. Wood entered the contest with a 13-game winning streak of his own. In the sixth inning with two out, Tris Speaker hit a ground rule double into part of the overflow crowd encircling the outfield and scored on another double by Duffy Lewis that barely eluded the grasp of Washington right fielder Danny Moeller. The Senators loaded the bases in the third inning and had runners on second base in the sixth, eighth and ninth, but Wood pitched out of the jam on each occasion. The shutout was Wood's third in succession. His winning streak reached 16 games, matching Johnson, before a 6-4 loss to the Tigers in Detroit on September 20. There have been only 10 winning streaks of 16 games or more in major league history. The record in a single season is 19 by Rube Marquard, also in 1912. Wood closed out the 1912 campaign with a 34-5 record (a club record), 35 complete games, 10 shutouts, 344 innings pitched, 258 strikeouts and a 1.91 ERA, all at the age of only 22.

# 07
## September

**O**n this date in 1923, Red Sox pitcher Howard Ehmke pitched a no-hitter for a 4-0 win over the Athletics in Philadelphia. There certainly was an element of luck involved. With two out in the sixth inning, opposing pitcher Slim Harriss drilled what looked to be a double to left field. Harriss failed to touch first base, however, and was declared out. The hit didn't count. In the eighth, Frank Welch hit a liner that left fielder Mike Menosky muffed. At first, the official scorer ruled it a hit, but within minutes reversed himself and called it an error. In the ninth inning, Ehmke retired Heinie Scheer on a ground out, Beauty McGowan on a fly ball to center and Wid Matthews on a grounder. Ehmke walked one and struck out one. Val Picinich was Ehmke's catcher during the no-hitter. Picinich caught three no-hitters with three different clubs during his career. The other two were Joe Bush's no-hitter with the Athletics in 1916 and Walter Johnson's with the Senators in 1920.

**08**
**September**

**T**he question of the day.
What happened when the
Red Sox traded Ken Harrelson?

The Red Sox traded Ken Harrelson,
Dick Ellsworth and Juan Pizarro to the
Indians for Sonny Siebert, Joe Azcue
and Vicente Romo on April 19, 1969. In
an attempt to nullify the trade, Harrelson
immediately announced his retirement. He
explained he couldn't leave Boston because of
outside business interests that earned him considerably more than
his $50,000 annual salary from the Red Sox. According to his agent,
Bob Wolff, the move from New England would cost Harrelson
$750,000. The trade was held up for three days before Harrelson
was placated when the Indians convinced him that business opportunities in Cleveland were equal to those in Boston and agreed
to double his salary. Red Sox fans were outraged at the trade of
Harrelson. Harrelson's cult following of young fans marched the
streets protesting the deal. Although he was only 27 at the time of
the trade, Harrelson played only 218 more big-league games and
hit only .220 with 33 homers in 719 at-bats.

# 09
## September

**T**he question of the day. What series is known in Red Sox lore as "The Boston Massacre." The 1978 Red Sox led the Yankees by 14 games on July 19. The advantage dwindled to four by the time the Yanks arrived at Fenway for a four-game series beginning on September 7. New York drew first blood by unleashing a 21-hit attack to stomp the Sox 15-3. On September 8, Boston committed seven errors and suffered a 13-2 loss at the hands of the Yankees. On September 9, the Yankees scored seven runs in the seventh inning and trounced the Red Sox 7-0. The big inning was sparked by a pop fly that landed amidst five Boston players. On September 10, the Yankees completed the sweep and moved into a tie for first place with a 7-4 decision. Manager Don Zimmer made a controversial choice in his starting pitcher in the key game by going with 22 year-old Bobby Sprowl, who was appearing in only his second big-league game. Sprowl didn't make it out of the first inning. He pitched only one more game with the Red Sox before being traded to the Astros. Sprowl pitched four years in the majors and never won a single game, finishing with an 0-3 record and a 5.44 ERA. Forever known as "The Boston Massacre," the Yankees outscored the Red Sox 42-9 in the four games. The Sox gave up 67 hits, collected only 21 and made 12 errors.

**10**
**September**

**O**n this day in 1918, the players of both the Cubs and the Boston Red Sox threatened to strike, delaying the start of game five of the World Series at Fenway Park. The players were angry because the winners' and losers' share of the gate receipts had been drastically reduced. The players' share that season was less than a third of what it had been in previous years. Attendance at the games was lower than normal because of World War I. Ticket prices were decreased, and baseball earmarked part of the gate money for wartime charities. Also the second-, third- and fourth-place clubs received part of the loot for the first time. Negotiations were held with the National Commission. The players wanted a guarantee of $2,000 to the winning team and $1,400 to the losing team, figures that were only a little more than half of what the participants in the 1917 Fall Classic received. The National Commission was unmoved. The players finally backed off their demands and threats to strike, not wanting to appear greedy while the nation was at war. The Cubs won 3-0. The Red Sox winning share of the Series was only $671 per player while the Cubs received just $1,103. In 1919, the winning and losing shares were $5,207 and $3,254, respectively.

# 11
# September

In his first start since pitching a no-hitter on September 7, Howard Ehmke one-hit the Yankees on this date in 1923 for a 3-0 win in New York. The only hit was a single by leadoff batter Whitey Witt in the first inning on a controversial scoring decision. Witt hit a bouncer to third baseman Howard Shanks, who fumbled the ball and threw too late to retire Witt at first base. After Witt's single, Ehmke retired 27 batters in a row. The official scorer who gave Witt the hit was Fred Lieb, one of the most respected sports-writers ever to cover baseball. The decision robbed Ehmke of back-to-back no-hitters and haunted Lieb until his death in 1980. Ehmke holds the American League record for fewest hits allowed in two consecutive complete game starts with one. At the major league level, only Johnny Vander Meer, with his back-to-back no-hitters with the Cincinnati Reds in 1938, has bettered Ehmke's achievement.

**12**
**September**

**O**n this date in 1979, Carl Yastrzemski collected his 3,000th hit in the eighth inning of a 9-2 win over the Yankees before 34,337 at Fenway Park. Facing Jim Beattie, Yaz reached the milestone with a single just past the outstretched glove of second baseman Willie Randolph. A mob of Red Sox teammates rushed the field to congratulate Yastrzemski. Reggie Jackson fielded the ball in right field and ran in to first base to hand the ball to Yaz. Microphones were brought onto the field, and Yastrzemski was honored in a 15-minute ceremony at first base. He was presented with a trophy as his father, Carl Yastrzemski, Sr., and his son Mike stood nearby. Earlier in the day, 50,000 jammed into Faneuil Hall Marketplace for "Carl Yastrzemski Day," which was proclaimed by Boston mayor Kevin White. Not to be outdone, Massachusetts governor Ed King proclaimed September 12 "Carl Yastrzemski Forever Day." The following day, Yaz went to Washington and had lunch with Speaker of the House Tip O'Neill. On October 5, Yaz went back to Washington to meet with President Jimmy Carter, who wanted to congratulate him for his 3,000th hit. The next day, Yastrzemski met Pope John Paul II at the White House.

# 13
## September

**O**n this date in 1946, the Red Sox broke a six-game losing streak and clinched their first AL pennant since 1918 with a 1-0 win over the Indians at League Park in Cleveland. The sole run in the game scored on the only inside-the-park home run of Ted Williams's career. Picking on a 3-1 pitch in the first inning, Williams foiled the Boudreau shift by hitting an opposite-field fly ball into empty left field and circled the bases before left fielder Pat Seerey could retrieve the ball, which rolled into a gutter along the distant left-field wall about 400 feet from home plate. Seerey had been stationed 20 feet behind the skinned portion of the infield. If he had been playing in a conventional defense, he probably would have caught the ball for the out. Williams's homer was one of only two hits off Cleveland pitcher Red Embree. Tex Hughson pitched the shutout for the Red Sox.

**B**

**14**
**September**

**O**n this date in 1923, Red Sox first baseman George Burns turned an unassisted triple play during a 4-3 win in 12 innings against the Indians at Fenway Park. With Riggs Stephenson on second base and Rube Lutzke on first in the second inning, Burns snared a liner off the bat of Frank Brower. Burns tagged Lutzke and raced to second, sliding into the bag ahead of Stephenson.

**B**

# 15
## September

**O**n this date in 1991, Roger Clemens survived an odd brushback battle to beat the Yankees 5-4 in New York. In the sixth inning, Matt Nokes was hit beneath the right shoulder with a fastball from Clemens. Nokes caught the ball under his armpit and, with a grimace, snapped the ball back at the Red Sox ace. Clemens caught the ball easily, and the two players began exchanging words. Players in both dugouts and bullpens poured onto the field, but there were no punches thrown and umpires kept the teams apart.

**B**

# 16
## September

On this date in 1965, Dave Morehead pitched a no-hitter to defeat the Indians 2-0 at Fenway Park. The only Cleveland base runner was Rocky Colavito, who walked leading off the second on a 3-2 pitch that was 12 inches outside. Morehead struck out eight. He faced three pinch-hitters in the ninth. Larry Brown was the first and belted a liner toward left field, but Sox shortstop Eddie Bressoud leaped and speared it. Lu Clinton followed by lining hard to Jim Gosger in center field. With two out, Vic Davalillo swung at an 0-2 pitch and hit a hopper toward the mound. Morehead tried to field the ball over his head, but it got away and landed about four feet behind him. He retrieved the ball, took a couple of steps toward first, stumbled momentarily and then threw toward Lee Thomas at first base. The throw was poorly aimed and too soft, but Thomas scooped it out of the dirt to retire Davalillo by a step. Paid attendance was only 1,247. Morehead was just 11 days past his 23rd birthday when he threw his no-hitter, but had little success in the majors, with a record of 12-20 over the remainder of his career. He didn't pitch another complete game until 1967.

B

# 17
## September

**D**uring a double-header against the Indians at Fenway Park on this date in 1931, Red Sox outfielder Earl Webb tied the all-time record for most doubles in a season, then broke it with his 65th two-bagger in the night-cap. The previous record of 64 was set by George Burns of the Indians in 1926. In the opener, the Red Sox scored seven runs in the first inning and won 9-2. Cleveland won the second game 2-1. Webb finished the 1931 season with 67 doubles, which is one of the strangest statistical flukes in baseball history. He tied and broke the record on his 34th birthday and prior to 1931 had never hit more than 30 doubles in a season. Webb entered the 1931 campaign with 55 lifetime major league doubles. His season high after 1931 was 28 in 1932, and he finished his career in 1933 with 155 doubles. No one has collected as many as 60 doubles in a season since 1936. The closest anyone has come to challenging Webb since 1936 was Todd Helton, who had 59 for the Rockies in 2000.

**B**

**18**
**September**

On this date in 1934, Bobo Newsom of the Browns held the Red Sox without a hit for nine innings, but Boston emerged with a ten-inning, 2-1 win in St. Louis. The Red Sox took a 1-0 lead in the second inning on two walks, an error and a fielder's choice. The Browns tied the game with a run in the sixth. In the 10th, Max Bishop and Billy Werber walked, and Bishop crossed the plate on Roy Johnson's single. Wes Ferrell was Boston's starting pitcher, but he was ejected while at the plate in the second inning for objecting too strenuously to the calls of home plate umpire Lou Kolls. Rick Ferrell joined in the conversation in defense of his brother and was also tossed. Rube Walberg pitched the final nine innings in relief for the Sox to earn the victory. Both Ferrell brothers were fined $100 for their ejection. In addition, Wes was suspended for five days and Rick for three.

# 19

## September

**O**n this date in 1945, there was trouble with some Fenway Park pigeons during an 11-10 and 3-0 double-header sweep of the Athletics. Red Sox outfielder Tom McBride took a bead on what he felt sure was a long fly ball off the bat of Sam Chapman but discovered too late that he was following the flight of a pigeon. The ball was hit behind him and clanged off the left-field wall for a double. Later, Boston's Skeeter Newsome hit a drive to left field for what appeared to be a sure double. Philadelphia outfielder Hal Peck picked up the ball and fired it toward the infield. It struck a pigeon in mid-flight and deflected to the second baseman, who tagged Newsome out.

B

**20
September**

**T**he question of the day.
What role did Tom Brunansky play in Red Sox lore?

The Red Sox won the AL East pennant on the last day of the 1990 with a 3-1 win over the White Sox, played on October 3 at Fenway Park. In the ninth inning, Chicago had runners on first and second with two outs when Tom Brunansky made a spectacular sliding catch off a drive by Ozzie Guillen in the right-field corner to end the game. The catch was made inches above the ground in a spot at Fenway Park that is out of the sight line of most of the fans in the ballpark. The contest was televised nationally on ESPN, and none of the network's cameras were able to catch Brunansky's grab because of the blind spot in that corner. Fortunately, first base umpire Tim McClellan saw the play. His out call was delayed, however, because he was struck by a frenzied fan who leaped onto the field in celebration.

# 21
## September

**T**ed Williams's fiery temper boiled over on this date in 1958 during a 2-0 win over the Senators at Fenway Park. Williams threw his bat 75 feet and struck 60-year-old Gladys Heffernan, who was the housekeeper of general manager Joe Cronin. Distressed after looking at a called third strike on a pitch from Bill Fischer, Williams flipped the bat in the air. Heffernan was seated in the first row and was hit by the knob end of the bat an inch above her left eye. Fighting back tears, Williams went over to console her. She suffered a contusion on the left side of her forehead and was hospitalized overnight as a precaution. Williams was fined $50 by AL president Will Harridge. The relatively low fine was in part due to Williams's obvious remorse over the incident. A week later, Williams became the oldest player in history to win a batting title. He turned 40 on August 30. Williams held the record until Barry Bonds led the NL in batting average in 2004, a little more than two months after celebrating his 40th birthday.

**B**

# 22
## September

**T**he question of the day. Who is the only player in major league history to hit grand slams from both sides of the plate in the same game?

Red Sox third baseman Bill Mueller became the only player in history to hit grand slams from both sides of the plate during a 14-7 win over the Rangers in Arlington on July 29, 2003. He hit three homers overall and drove in nine runs. Batting left-handed, Mueller hit a solo homer off R. A. Dickey in the third inning. Hitting from the right side in the seventh, Mueller blasted a grand slam facing Aaron Fultz. An inning later, Mueller connected again for his second grand slam, this one facing lefty Jay Powell. There have been 12 players in baseball history with two grand slams in a game, and four have been members of the Red Sox. The other three are Jim Tabor (July 4, 1939), Rudy York (July 27, 1946) and Nomar Garciaparra (May 10, 1999). Mueller also won the AL batting title in 2003 in one of the closest races in history. On the final day of the season, Mueller was 0-for-1 as a pinch-hitter during a 3-1 loss to the Devil Rays in St. Petersburg on September 28 to finish the year with a .326 average. Teammate Manny Ramirez, who sat out the final contest, just missed his second straight batting title, finishing at .325. Derek Jeter was hitless in three at-bats the same day to end the season at .324.

# 23
## September

**W**ith Vice President Richard Nixon in attendance, Ted Williams set a major league record for most consecutive plate appearances with 16 over six games during a 9-4 win over the Senators in Washington. He reached base five times in five plate appearances with a single, three walks and a hit batsman. The streak is all the more remarkable when one considers that Williams was 39 years old and had just recovered from a bout of pneumonia. It started on September 17 in his first appearance since September 1 with a pinch-hit homer during a 9-8 win over the Athletics at Fenway. The streak ended on September 24 when he grounded out against Hal Griggs of the Senators in his first plate appearance of a 2-1 win over the Senators. Griggs finished his career with a 6-26 career record and a 5.50 ERA.

# 24 September

On this date in 1919, Babe Ruth hit his 28th homer of the season, breaking the existing record of 27 set by Ned Williamson of the Cubs in 1884. The Red Sox lost 2-1 in 13 innings to the Yankees in New York. Sox pitcher Waite Hoyt retired 34 consecutive Yankee batters from the second through the thirteenth before taking the loss. Four days earlier, Ruth hit home run number 27 on "Babe Ruth Day" at Fenway Park. The Sox won 4-3 and 5-4 in a double-header against the White Sox before 31,000. In between games, Ruth was feted by the Knights of Columbus, who gave him $600 worth of United States Treasury certificates, cuff links, a fountain pen, a box of cigars, a traveling bag and a pair of new baseball spikes. No one, except perhaps team owner Harry Frazee, knew that this was Ruth's last appearance as a member of the Red Sox at Fenway. In January 1920, Frazee sold Ruth to the Yankees.

# 25
## September

**T**he question of the day.

How did an injury to Duane Josephson change the history of the Red Sox?

Duane Josephson started the first three games of the 1972 season at catcher, but was shelved because of a pulled muscle. Bob Montgomery started the fourth game, but the Indians stole four bases on him. Manager Eddie Kasko then turned to rookie Carlton Fisk, saying, "Fisk may be inexperienced, but at least he can throw." The Red Sox considered Fisk to be more of a defensive weapon than an offensive threat. In 592 at-bats at Class AAA, he hit 22 homers but batted only .247. Fisk was an immediate sensation in the majors, however, and by mid-season he had performed well enough to make the All-Star team. By the end of the season, he had a .293 average and a league-leading nine triples, 28 doubles, 22 homers and a .538 slugging percentage. Fisk won the Rookie of the Year Award by a unanimous vote, was fourth in the MVP balloting and earned a Gold Glove. By the time his career was over in 1993, Fisk had caught more games than anyone in history, hit one of the most dramatic home runs in World Series annals and accounted for more home runs than any other catcher until Mike Piazza passed him in 2004. Fisk was elected to the Hall of Fame in 2000 in his second year on the ballot.

# 26
## September

**O**n this date in 1949, the Red Sox took a one-game lead in the AL pennant race by winning a thrilling 7-6 decision over the Yankees before 67,434 on a Monday afternoon in New York. The Sox trailed 6-3 before exploding for four runs in the eighth inning. The winning run scored when Bobby Doerr executed a squeeze bunt that brought in Johnny Pesky from third base. The throw from first baseman Tommy Henrich to catcher Ralph Houk beat Pesky by several yards, but umpire Bill Grieve called Pesky safe. Houk and manager Casey Stengel argued long and loud that Pesky was out, to no avail. After the game, Yankee outfielder Cliff Mapes asked Grieve how much he bet on the game and had to be restrained from punching the umpire. Stengel, Mapes and Houk were all fined by AL president Will Harridge. It was Boston's 10th win in a row and marked the first time the Yankees had been out of first place all year. The Sox were 35-36 and 12 games out of first on July 4 and looked to be hopelessly out of the race. "That's it," declared Stengel. "The Red Sox won't bother us." The Sox won 61 of their next 81 games, however. In the end though, the Yankees prevailed. The Sox entered the final two games of the season with a one-game lead, but lost 5-4 and 5-3 at Yankee Stadium to blow the pennant.

# 27

## September

**O**n this date in 1905, Bill Dinneen pitched a no-hitter to defeat the White Sox 2-0 in the first game of a double-header at Huntington Grounds. Dinneen, who had been sidelined by a sore arm, was making his first appearance since August 31. He walked two and struck out six. After easily retiring Fielder Jones and Frank Isbell, Dinneen induced George Davis to pop up to third baseman Bob Unglaub for the final out. With Cy Young starting the second game, the White Sox took revenge by erupting for nine runs in the first inning and five in the second, winning 15-1. The game ended after six innings due to darkness. Dinneen is the only individual to pitch a no-hitter and umpire in another. During his 29 seasons as an American League umpire from 1909 through 1937, Dinneen officiated in eight no-hitters. A pitcher with a 172-176 lifetime record, he was also the hero of the first World Series, played in 1903 against the Pirates. Dinneen won three games for Boston, including two shutouts. His 28 strikeouts remained a World Series record until it was broken by Bob Gibson in 1964. As an umpire, Dinneen worked in 45 World Series games.

**28
September**

On this date in 1941, Ted Williams collected six hits in eight at-bats during a double-header against the Athletics at Shibe Park to finish the season with a batting average of .406. No one since has hit over .400 in a season. Batting averages are rounded off to the nearest thousandth of a decimal point, and Williams entered the day with an average of .39955, which rounds off to .400. Manager Joe Cronin gave Williams the option of sitting out the September 28 games to preserve his .400 average, but Williams insisted on playing. To put his average above .400 in the season-ending double-header, Williams needed at least three hits in a minimum of seven at-bats, or four hits in nine a-bats or fewer. Philadelphia manager Connie Mack told his pitchers to do all they could to get Williams out, but to throw strikes. Mack didn't want his pitchers being accused of keeping Williams from reaching the .400 mark by issuing walks. In the first game, won by the Red Sox 12-11, Williams erased all doubt about finishing above .400 with a single in the second inning, a homer in the fifth, a single in the sixth and another single in the seventh in his first four plate appearances. He reached on an error in the ninth.

**B**

# 29
## September

**T**he question of the day.

How did an exhibition game hamper the Red Sox' chances of winning the 1946 World Series?

The 1946 regular season ended on September 29 with the World Series scheduled to start on October 2. The National League pennant race ended in a tie, however, between the Dodgers and the Cardinals. The two clubs met in a best-of-three playoff to determine the league champion, which pushed back the start of the Fall Classic to October 6. To keep his team fresh during the layoff, manager Joe Cronin arranged for the Sox to play three exhibition games against a team of American League all-stars that included Joe DiMaggio, Hank Greenberg and Luke Appling. In the game on October 1, Ted Williams was hit squarely on the elbow by a pitch from Mickey Haefner of the Senators. In excruciating pain, Williams went to the hospital for x-rays, which turned out to be negative. After this unfortunate injury, the last two games against the all-stars were canceled. Williams's elbow swelled to three times its normal size and hampered his swing throughout the Series. The Red Sox entered the World Series against the Cardinals as 3-1 favorites, but lost in seven games. Williams had five hits, all singles, in 25 at-bats.

**B**

**30 September**

**T**he question of the day.

Why is Johnny Pesky blamed for the seventh-game loss to the Cardinals in the 1946 World Series?

Dom Dimaggio had just tied the score 3-3 in the eighth inning of the deciding seventh game. But DiMaggio sprained his ankle and was replaced by Culberson in center field. Joe Cronin also made a controversial pitching choice in the fateful eighth. Joe Dobson was lifted for a pinch-hitter in the top of the inning: Cronin went with Bob Klinger, who hadn't pitched in three weeks after being away from the club because of a family illness. Enos Slaughter led off the inning with a single, but Klinger retired the next two hitters. Harry Walker was up next for the Cards, hitting a drive to the outfield. Culberson fielded the ball and threw to shortstop Johnny Pesky. Slaughter, sprinting all the way, was just rounding third base when Pesky received the ball with his back to the infield. Pesky didn't suspect that Slaughter would be dashing for the plate and pulled the ball down slightly while turning toward the plate. The Sox shortstop was surprised to see Slaughter heading home and needed an additional second to get into position to make a quick throw, which was up the line. Slaughter scored easily and the Cards had a 4-3 lead that held up for the world championship when the Red Sox didn't score in the ninth.

**B**

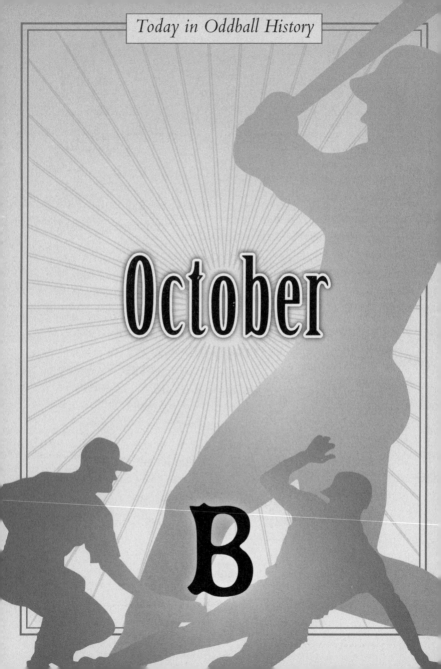

# October

# B

**01**
October

**O**n this date in 1903, the first game of the first modern World Series was played. The Pirates defeated the Red Sox 7-3 before 16,242 at Huntington Grounds as Pittsburgh's Deacon Phillippe outdueled Cy Young. The American League, and the Red Sox, were formed in 1901 and immediately began raiding National League rosters for talent. A two-year war raged as each league tried to lure players to the other organization with a promise of higher salaries. A peace agreement was reached in January 1903 that brought an end to the raids and opened the way to a postseason series. When it became apparent in mid-August that the Red Sox and Pirates would win pennants in their respective leagues, Pittsburgh owner Barney Dreyfuss issued a challenge to Sox owner Henry Killilea to hold a World Series. In early September they decided on a best-of-nine format. The players, whose contracts expired on September 30, would receive two weeks additional pay plus a share of the gate receipts. The Red Sox won the Series and went on to take titles again in 1912, 1915, 1916 and 1918.

**B**

# 02
## October

**O**n this date in 1949, the last day of the regular season, the Red Sox blew a chance to win the AL pennant. The Sox came to New York for a closing two-game series against the Yankees needing only one win to advance to the World Series. The Red Sox lost on October 2 with a 5-3 defeat that allowed the Yanks to reach the Fall Classic. Trailing 1-0 in the eighth, Red Sox manager Joe McCarthy made the controversial decision to lift starting pitcher Ellis Kinder for pinch-hitter Tom Wright, a rookie outfielder with only six at-bats in the majors. Wright walked, but was erased when Dom DiMaggio hit into a double play. Mel Parnell, who started the previous day, took the mound in the last half of the inning and yielded a homer to Tommy Henrich and a single to Yogi Berra. Parnell was relieved by Tex Hughson, who gave up three more runs on a two-out, bases-loaded double to Jerry Coleman for a 5-0 Yankee advantage. Right fielder Al Zarilla, who many believe was playing too deep, just missed a shoestring catch on Coleman's drive. The Red Sox rallied desperately in the ninth for three runs before Yankee pitcher Vic Raschi could retire the side. The Yankees beat the Brooklyn Dodgers in five games in the World Series.

**03**
October

**G**ame three of the first World Series, played on this date in 1903, nearly ended because of a riot at Huntington Grounds in Boston. The official attendance was announced as 18,801, but it's estimated that as many as 25,000 were inside the enclosure, which had only about 9,000 seats. Many climbed the outfield fences and scrambled into the ballpark for free. Fans were placed behind ropes in the deepest parts of the outfield, but began inching forward, first a few people at a time, then a stampede. The 50 policemen on hand were powerless to keep the fans behind the ropes. As the fans packed the field, the police tried moving them from the infield, using baseball bats. At first the crowd was good-natured, but the brute force of the police whacking them with wooden bats roused their ire. The angry mob hacked to pieces a water hose that had been brought out to assist in qelling the crowd. A reserve force of police swinging billy clubs indiscriminately and using rubber hoses succeeding in moving the crowd far enough back to play the game, but fans were stationed only about 50 yards beyond the infield. Balls hit into the crowd were ground rule doubles. The Pirates won the game 4-2.

# 04
## October

**O**n this date in 1948, the Indians defeated the Red Sox 8-3 in a one-game playoff to decide the AL champion before 33,957 at Fenway Park. Indians player-manager Lou Boudreau sent rookie Gene Bearden, pitching on one day of rest, to the mound against Denny Galehouse of the Red Sox. Bearden, supported by two homers and two singles from Boudreau, pitched a complete game and allowed only one earned run. Galehouse was removed with none out in the fourth inning after allowing a three-run homer to Ken Keltner, which broke a 1-1 tie. Reliever Ellis Kinder couldn't hold the Indians either, allowing four runs and eight hits in six innings. The Indians moved on to win the World Series in six games against the Boston Braves. McCarthy's inexplicable choice of Galehouse to start the crucial playoff game has long been a sore point with Red Sox fans. Boston's starting rotation during the final week of the season consisted of Kinder, Mel Parnell, Jack Kramer and Joe Dobson. Kinder had four days of rest and Parnell three. Kinder was riding a five-game winning streak. Yet, McCarthy chose the 36-year-old Galehouse, who hadn't started a game since September 18, when he allowed four runs and six hits in 3⅔ innings to the lowly Browns.

**B**

**05**
**October**

**O**n this date in 1967, Jim Lonborg pitched a one-hitter in game two of the World Series to defeat the Cardinals 5-0 before 35,186 at Fenway Park. He retired the first 19 batters he faced before walking Curt Flood. The only St. Louis hit was a two-out double by Julian Javier in the eighth inning. Carl Yastrzesmki hit two homers and a single and drove in four runs. Lonborg took the mound again on October 9 in game five and pitched a three-hitter for a 3-1 victory over Steve Carlton in St. Louis. Lonborg set a World Series record for the fewest hits allowed in consecutive complete-game World Series starts with four. He lost the shutout when Roger Maris hit a homer with two outs in the ninth. Lonborg came back to pitch the deciding game seven against Bob Gibson on October 12. Pitching on only two days' rest, Lonborg had nothing left and went six innings, giving up seven runs, six of them earned, and 10 hits. The "Impossible Dream" season ended with a 7-2 loss at Fenway Park.

**B**

# 06
## October

**O**n this date in 2003, The Red Sox advance to the Championship Series against the Yankees. After losing the first two games of the American League Division Series to the Athletics, the Red Sox won their third in a row with a 4-3 decision in Oakland. The Sox trailed 1-0 before a four-run rally in the sixth. Jason Varitek led off the inning with a homer. After Johnny Damon walked and Todd Walker was hit by a pitch, Manny Ramirez belted a three-run homer off Barry Zito. The A's scored a run in their half of the sixth and another in the eighth off Pedro Martinez before a succession of four relievers nailed down the victory. Derek Lowe struck out the final two batters, both looking, with the tying run on third. There was a scary moment in the seventh inning when Damon and second baseman Damian Jackson collided head-to-head while chasing Jermaine Dye's fly ball. Jackson shook it off, but Damon was knocked unconscious with a concussion and left the field in an ambulance. He missed the first two games of the ALCS.

**B**

**07**
October

**T**he question of the day.

Who was Henry Killilea?

Henry Killilea was an attorney from Milwaukee who purchased the Red Sox from original owner Charles Somers in January 1903. Despite winning the first World Series in 1903, Killilea was vilified in the Boston newspapers for his absentee ownership and skinflint operation. Many accused him of selling the best seats at Huntington Grounds to scalpers during the World Series in exchange for a portion of the profits. It didn't help his relationship with the media when Killilea charged admission to writers covering the event. He even made Pittsburgh Pirates owner Barney Dreyfuss pay for a ticket. The reserve players on the Boston club had to work to take tickets, even Cy Young. During game three, Young was in his street clothes in the Red Sox office counting the gate receipts when he was summoned to pitch after starting Long Tom Hughes lasted only two innings. Dreyfuss donated a larger share of the profits to his athletes than Killilea, and as a result, the Pirates received $1,316 for losing the World Series while the Red Sox garnered $1,186 for winning. The controversy forced Killilea to sell to club the following April.

# 08
## October

**O**n this date in 1904, a crowd of nearly 30,000 shoehorned their way into Huntington Grounds to watch the Red Sox take a double-header and regain first place from the Yankees with 13-2 and 1-0 victories. Yankee pitcher Jack Chesbro, starting for the second day in a row, wasn't up to the challenge and was shelled in the opener. There was no break between the two games because of concerns about daylight. Yankee left fielder Patsy Dougherty, who made the last out of the first game, was the leadoff hitter in the second tilt and stayed at the plate while Bill Dinneen walked off the field and Cy Young took the mound. The nightcap was called by darkness after seven innings. The only run of the contest was scored in the fifth on an error by Yankee third baseman Wid Conroy, one of three he made during the game. It was Young's third consecutive shutout and his 26th win of the season. After the games, fans carried the Sox players off the field on their shoulders, and thousands remained until the players had donned their street clothes and then cheered them on the way to their homes. The wins meant that the Red Sox only had to win once in their season-ending double-header against the Yankees on October 10 to take the AL pennant.

**09**
**October**

**O**n this date in 1916, Babe Ruth led the Red Sox to a 14-inning, 2-1 win over the Dodgers in Boston in a pitching duel with Sherry Smith. The Dodgers scored in the first inning on an inside-the-park homer by Hi Myers, and the Red Sox countered with a tally in the third on Everett Scott's triple and a ground out by Ruth. For the next 10 innings, Ruth and Smith matched zeroes. With darkness rapidly settling over the field, Dick Hoblitzel led off the Boston half of the 14th inning by drawing his fourth walk of the game. He scored on a double by pinch-hitter Del Gainor. The 14-inning encounter was the longest in World Series history until it was tied in game three in 2005 when the White Sox beat the Astros 7-5 in 14 innings in Houston. The Red Sox-Dodgers clash was played at Braves Field, not Fenway Park. It was the third year in a row in which Boston hosted a World Series, and the third in a row in which the Boston club did not play in its home park. The Braves played at Fenway Park in 1914 because it had a larger capacity than South End Grounds, where the NL club played their home games. Braves Field, which held over 40,000 fans, opened in August 1915 and was used by the Red Sox in the World Series in both 1915 and 1916.

# 10
## October

**O**n this date in 1904, the Red Sox clinched the AL pennant with a 3-2 win in the first game of a double-header at Hilltop Park in New York. The crowd in the outfield stood 12 to 15 deep. The Yankees' Jack Chesbro, who pitched 445 innings in 1904 and was making his third start in four days, faced Bill Dinneen, who had pitched a complete game only two days earlier. The Yankees scored first with two runs in the fifth, the second on a bases-loaded walk, but the Red Sox evened the score with a pair in the seventh on a throwing error by New York second baseman Jimmy Williams. Lou Criger, one of the slowest players of the era, began the ninth inning with an infield single on a slow roller to shortstop Kid Elberfield. Criger advanced to second on Dinneen's sacrifice and to third on Kip Selbach's groundout. Criger scored the deciding tally when Chesbro launched a wild pitch far over the head of catcher Red Kleinow with two out and two strikes on Freddie Parent to give the Sox a 3-2 lead. In the New York ninth, Dinneen struck out John Ganzel, walked Wid Conroy, retired Kleinow on a pop-up to second baseman Hobe Ferris, and walked Deacon McGuire, who was pinch-hitting for Chesbro. The game ended when Patsy Dougherty, who started the season as a member of the Red Sox, swung and missed on Dinneen's 2-2 pitch.

**11**
**October**

In a matchup of Pedro Martinez and Roger Clemens on this date in 2003, the Yankees took a two-games-to-one lead in the ALCS with a 4-3 win over the Red Sox before 34,209 at Fenway Park. The game will long be remembered for the altercation between the 31-year-old Martinez and 72-year-old Yankee coach Don Zimmer and a scuffle in the bullpen between a groundskeeper and two Yankees, adding a bizarre chapter in baseball's most bitter rivalry. The fight began after Martinez threw behind Karim Garcia's head in the fourth inning, and Clemens threw a high pitch to Manny Ramirez. The Red Sox outfielder veered toward the mound, and both benches cleared. Zimmer lunged at Martinez, who sidestepped him, grabbed him by the head and tossed him to the ground. Zimmer landed face down and rolled on his back, suffering a cut on his head. In the ninth a fight erupted between Fenway groundskeeper Paul Williams and Yankee players Garcia and Jeff Nelson. Williams contended that Garcia and Nelson attacked him. According to Nelson, Williams was waving a rally flag in the Yankee bullpen. Williams acknowledged pumping his fist twice while holding a white towel after the Red Sox turned a double play in the ninth. Later, Boston police charged Williams, Garcia and Nelson with assault and battery, but prosecutors dropped the charges.

# 12
## October

**O**n the brink of elimination, the Red Sox scored a breathtaking 7-6 win over the Angels in 11 innings in Anaheim on this date in 1986. The Sox came into the game trailing the best-of-seven series three games to one and were behind 5-2 leading into the ninth. Bill Buckner led off the inning with a single. One out later, Don Baylor hit a two-run homer to cut the lead to 5-4. Dwight Evans popped up for the second out. California manager Gene Mauch brought in Gary Lucas to face Rich Gedman, who was hit with Lucas's first pitch. It was the first time that Lucas hit a batter in four years. Lucas was replaced by Donnie Moore to face Dave Henderson. Moore had a 1-2 count on Henderson, putting the Angels one strike away from the World Series. After a ball on a low pitch, Henderson fouled off two deliveries and lined a homer into the left-field seats for a 6-5 Boston lead, but the Angels tied the game in the bottom half. Moore was still pitching in the 11th when the Sox scored the winning run. Boston loaded the bases when Baylor was hit by a pitch, and Dwight Evans and Gedman singled. Henderson hit a sacrifice fly into center field. The Red Sox closed out the ALCS by defeating the Angels at Fenway Park 10-4 in game six and 8-1 in game seven. The Sox moved on to the World Series, only to lose games six and seven to the Mets.

**13**
October

**T**he question of the day.
Why was there no World
Series in 1904?

The Red Sox won the AL pennant
and the New York Giants took the NL
crown in 1904, but there was no World
Series because Giants owner John Brush
and manager John McGraw refused to
participate. Brush and McGraw both held
long-standing grudges against AL president
Ban Johnson. A particular sore point was the establishment of
the Yankees in New York in 1903. Brush and McGraw indignantly
dismissed the AL as a "minor league" even though the Red Sox
defeated the Pirates in the 1903 World Series. Red Sox players and
fans were not the only ones who were angry over the failure to
defend their world championship on the field. The actions of Brush
and McGraw also cost the Giants players a significant wad of cash.
*The Sporting News* declared the Red Sox world champions by
default. Brush and McGraw were roasted in the press for months
all across the nation for their refusal to compete in the postseason.
To add a bizarre twist to the saga, Brush proposed rules govern-
ing future World Series that were passed by the owners of the two
leagues in January 1905. Among the stipulations was a $10,000 fine
for any club that refused to play in the Series in the future. Many of
these rules are still in effect.

# 14
## October

**T**he Reds won a controversial game three of the 1975 World Series on this date by beating the Red Sox 6-5 in 10 innings at Riverfront Stadium in Cincinnati. The Reds had a 5-1 lead after five innings, but the Red Sox battled back with a run in the sixth, another in the seventh and two more in the ninth. Cesar Geronimo led off the Cincinnati 10th with a single to center field. Pinch-hitter Ed Armbrister then bunted in front of the plate and bumped into Carlton Fisk as the Red Sox catcher fielded the ball. Fisk threw the ball into center field in an attempt to retire Geronimo at second base. Geronimo moved on to third base and Armbrister to second on the play. Home plate umpire Larry Barnett ruled there was no interference on Armbrister's part, despite furious protests from the Red Sox. After Pete Rose was walked intentionally, Joe Morgan hit a fly ball over Fred Lynn's head to score Geronimo with the winning run.

**B**

**15**
**October**

**G**ame seven of the 1912 World Series was delayed for nearly half an hour on this date because of a ticket snafu involving the Royal Rooters, a devoted Red Sox fan club of about 300. Heading into the contest, the Red Sox had three victories in the Series, the Giants two, with another game ending in a tie. The Royal Rooters sat together at games in Boston and often followed the club on the road. According to tradition, the group marched into Fenway Park about five minutes before the start of the game with a large banner headed by their band, which played the song "Tessie." The Royal Rooters then made their way to their seats, which had been reserved for them next to the Red Sox bench. Before game seven, the Royal Rooters found their usual seats occupied. The group broke onto the playing field just as the game started and made plans to raid the grandstand and forcibly remove those who had taken their seats. The Royal Rooters were stopped by a squad of mounted policemen and were kept behind a rope in the outfield, where they had to stand throughout the contest. The rest of the crowd reacted angrily to the actions of the police against the Royal Rooters. Red Sox starter Smoky Joe Wood allowed six runs in the first inning, in part because his arm stiffened during the delay, and the Giants won 11-4.

# 16
## October

**O**n this date in 2003, the Red Sox suffered an agonizing 6-5 game-seven loss to the Yankees at Yankee Stadium, costing Boston a shot at the World Series. The starting pitchers were Pedro Martinez and Roger Clemens. The Sox took a 3-0 lead in the second inning. Trot Nixon hit a two-run homer, followed by a double from Jason Varitek, who scored on an error. Kevin Millar homered on the first pitch of the fourth inning to make it 4-0. Jason Giambi homered for the Yanks in the fifth and seventh to close the game to 4-2. A David Ortiz home run in the eighth off David Wells gave the Red Sox a little breathing room with a 5-2 advantage. Martinez was still on the mound when the Yankees came to bat in the eighth. Grady Little's decision to leave Martinez in the game will remain a source of controversy for decades. Pedro had shown signs of weakening, giving up a homer and a single in the seventh. Up to that point, the bullpen had been brilliant, allowing only two runs in 31 innings in the playoffs. After retiring the first batter of the eighth, Martinez gave up four straight hits, tying the score 5-5. Finally, Little pulled Martinez and brought in Alan Embree. It was still 5-5 when Aaron Boone homered on the first pitch of the 11th inning from Tim Wakefield and crushed the hopes of the Red Sox Nation once more.

**B**

**17**
**October**

**O**n this date in 2004, the Red Sox stayed alive with a thrilling 12-inning, 6-4 win over the Yankees before 35,120 at Fenway Park. Coming into the game, the Sox trailed the Yankees three games to none in the ALCS. The Sox were behind 2-0 before scoring three times in the fifth. David Ortiz put Boston ahead with a two-out, two-run single. The Yankees quickly got the lead back with a pair in the sixth. It was still 4-3 Yankees heading into the ninth with Mariano Rivera on the mound. Rivera entered the game with a 0.69 ERA in 104⅓ postseason innings. Kevin Millar led off the inning with a walk. Dave Roberts pinch-ran for Millar and stole second. Bill Mueller singled to bring Roberts across the plate and tie the score. The Sox loaded the bases, but Ortiz popped up to end the inning. Ortiz made amends in the 12th, however, by hitting a two-run, walk-off homer off Paul Quantrill on a 2-1 pitch with no outs after Manny Ramirez led off the inning with a single.

# 18
## October

**O**n this date in 2004, David Ortiz provided an extra-inning walk-off hit for the second night in a row to lead the Red Sox to a 5-4 win over the Yankees in 14 innings before 35,120 at Fenway Park in game five of the ALCS. The Sox took a 2-0 lead in the first off Jason Varitek, but the Yankees responded with a run in the second and three in the sixth for a 4-2 advantage. It was still 4-2 heading into the eighth, and the Sox were six outs from elimination. Ortiz led off with a homer off Tom Gordon. A walk to Kevin Millar, a single by Trot Nixon and a sacrifice fly by Jason Varitek tied the score 4-4. The game remained deadlocked 4-4 until the 14th inning. Johnny Damon walked with one out, and Manny Ramirez drew a pass on a full count with two down. Ortiz followed with his game-winning hit. The contest lasted five hours and 49 minutes.

**B**

# 19
## October

On this date in 2004, the Red Sox evened the ALCS at three games apiece by defeating the Yankees 4-2 at Yankee Stadium. The game was scoreless when the Red Sox crossed the plate four times in the fourth. Jason Varitek singled in the first run, and Mark Bellhorn closed out the scoring with a three-run homer. Left-field umpire Jim Joyce originally ruled Bellhorn's homer "in play." The ruling was overturned after Joyce conferred with the other five umpires, who saw the ball hit a spectator just beyond the outfield wall. A Yankee rally was cut short in the eighth when Alex Rodriguez was called out for interference by swatting the ball out of Bronson Arroyo's glove on a tag play on the first-base line. Curt Schilling went seven innings and allowed only one run on four hits.

**B**

# 20
## October

On this date in 2004, the Red Sox completed their incredible comeback over the Yankees in the ALCS and advanced to the World Series against the Cardinals by winning game seven 10-3 at Yankee Stadium. The Sox put the game away early. David Ortiz hit a two-run homer in the first off Kevin Brown, and Johnny Damon clouted a grand slam against Javier Vasquez in the second to put Boston ahead 6-0. Damon also hit a two-run homer in the fourth facing Vasquez, and Mark Bellhorn homered in the eighth. Pitching on two days' rest, Derek Lowe allowed one run and one hit in six innings.

B

# 21
## October

**O**n this date in 1975, the Red Sox won a thrilling sixth game of the World Series 7-6 in 12 innings over the Reds at Fenway Park. Heading into the contest, the Reds held a three-games-to-two edge in the Series. The Sox struck first on a three-run, first-inning home run by Fred Lynn off Gary Nolan. Luis Tiant held the Reds scoreless until the fifth when Ken Griffey, Sr. hit a triple off the center-field wall to score two runs. Cincinnati took a 5-3 lead in the seventh on George Foster's two-run double. Cesar Geronimo's eighth-inning homer made it 6-3, and the Sox were six outs away from elimination. But in the Boston eighth, Bernie Carbo hit a two-out, three-run, pinch-homer into the center-field bleachers. The Sox loaded the bases in the ninth inning with no outs, but couldn't score. In the 11th, right fielder Dwight Evans made a leaping catch in right field to rob Joe Morgan of a home run, then fired the ball back to the infield to complete an inning-ending double play. At 12:34 a.m., Carlton Fisk led off the bottom of the 12th by hitting a Pat Darcy pitch off the left-field foul pole to win the game 7-6 and tie the Series three games apiece. As Fisk rounded the bases, organist John Kiley boomed the opening notes of Handel's "Hallelujah Chorus."

# 22
## October

**O**n this date in 1975, the Red Sox blew a 3-0 lead and lost game seven of the World Series 4-3 to the Reds before 35,205 at Fenway Park on a run in the ninth. The Sox scored all three of their runs in the third inning off Don Gullett, the first on a single by Carl Yastrzemski and the last two on bases-loaded walks to Rico Petrocelli and Dwight Evans. The Cincinnati comeback started in the sixth. With Johnny Bench on second and two out, Tony Perez hit a Lee "blooper pitch" over the Green Monster to make the score 3-2. In the seventh, Ken Griffey, Sr. walked and stole second. Roger Moret replaced Lee and recorded two outs. The Red Sox were just seven outs from a world championship when Moret issued a walk to Ed Armbrister and a single to Pete Rose to tie the score. In the ninth, with rookie Jim Burton on the mound for the Sox, Griffey walked again and went to second on a sacrifice. With two out and the count 1-2, Joe Morgan's shallow single to center scored Griffey to give the Reds a 4-3 lead. Will McEnaney retired the Sox in order in the ninth, the last out on a fly ball to center field hit by Carl Yastrzemski. Burton, who gave up the winning run in the ninth, pitched only one more big-league game.

**B**

# 23
## October

**T**he question of the day.
Who was the first player in World Series history to hit two homers in a game?

In the second game of the 1903 World Series, played on October 2 in Boston, Red Sox outfielder Patsy Dougherty became the first player in the history of the Fall Classic to hit a lead-off homer and the first to homer twice in a game. Dougherty led off the first inning with an inside-the-park homer to deep right-center off Pittsburgh's Sam Leever. Dougherty homered again in the seventh over the left-field fence off reliever Bucky Veil. Only one ball had been hit over that fence during the regular season. The outburst wasn't typical of Dougherty's career. He hit only 17 regular-season homers in 4,558 at-bats. Dougherty is the only player with fewer than 40 career homers to hit two in a Series game, and it was the only time he hit more than one in a game. No one else homered in World Series play until 1908.

# 24
## October

**O**n this date in 2007, the Red Sox opened the World Series with a 13-1 win over the Colorado Rockies at Fenway Park. Dustin Pedroia, in his first World Series, led off the first inning with a home run from Jeff Francis. The Sox added two more runs in the first inning, one in the second, two in the fourth and seven in the fifth. Eight Boston doubles tied a World Series record. Kevin Youkilis and David Ortiz each hit two doubles, and Manny Ramirez, Mike Lowell, Jason Varitek and J. D. Drew hit one each. Eight different Red Sox batters drove in a run and eight scored. In seven innings, Josh Beckett struck out nine batters, including the first four he faced. The game was the fourth consecutive rout by the Sox. In the ALCS, the club trailed the Indians three games to one before winning three in a row by scores of 7-1, 12-2 and 11-2. Over four consecutive postseason games, the Sox outscored the opposition 43-6. The Sox completed the sweep of the Rockies by winning 2-1, 10-5 and 4-3 to capture their second world championship in four years. The Rockies entered the Series with 21 wins in their last 22 games.

**25**
**October**

**T**he infamous game six of the 1986 World Series against the Mets at Shea Stadium was played on this date. The Red Sox took a two-run lead into the bottom of the 10th inning and were twice within one strike of a world championship only to suffer a crushing 6-5 defeat. Dave Henderson homered in the top of the 10th to give the Sox a 4-3 advantage. With two out, Wade Boggs lined a double to left-center and scored on a single by Marty Barrett, bringing the score to 5-3. Calvin Schiraldi retired the first two New York batters in the bottom half. The first world championship for Boston since 1918 seemed to be a certainty. But a bizarre turnaround was about to take place. Gary Carter started the string of improbable events by lining a single to left. Pinch-hitter Kevin Mitchell singled to center. Schiraldi got two strikes on Ray Knight, but Knight looped an 0-2 pitch to center, scoring Carter and sending Mitchell to third. Bob Stanley relieved Schiraldi. The Sox were again one strike from the championship when Stanley bounced a 2-2 pitch to Mookie Wilson to the screen. Mitchell scored to tie the game 5-5, and Knight went to second. On the next pitch, Wilson bounced a routine grounder to first baseman Bill Buckner, but Buckner let the ball get under his glove and through his legs, and Knight crossed the plate with the winning run.

# 26
## October

**O**n this date in 1986, game seven of the World Series between the Red Sox and Mets at Shea Stadium was rained out: the Sox' chance to redeem themselves for the agonizing game six loss was pushed back 24 hours. The game was played on October 27. Boston took a 3-0 lead into the bottom of the sixth inning, but lost 8-5. The Sox scored three times in the second. Dwight Evans and Rich Gedman hit back-to-back homers off Ron Darling, and another run scored on a single by Wade Boggs. Bruce Hurst allowed only one New York base runner through the first five innings but tired in the sixth. Darryl Strawberry hit a bases-loaded single for the first two runs. The tying run scored when Evans, in right field, tried for a diving catch on Gary Carter's blooper but couldn't control the ball. Calvin Schiraldi replaced Hurst in the seventh, and Ray Knight greeted him with a homer to put the Mets ahead 4-3. The Mets added two more runs in the inning off Al Nipper to go ahead 6-3. The Red Sox added two runs in the eighth on a double by Evans, but the Mets countered with two in their half to take an 8-5 advantage. In the ninth, Jesse Orosco retired the Sox in order. Marty Barrett struck out to end the game. The 1986 Red Sox are the only team in history to be one strike away from a world championship and come up empty.

**27**
October

**O**n this date in 2004, the Red Sox shut out the Cardinals 3-0 in St. Louis for their first world championship since 1918. The Sox entered the contest with a three-games-to-none lead after beating the Cards 11-9, 6-2 and 4-1. Johnny Damon led off the first inning with a homer. It was the fourth game in a row that the Sox scored in the first. Trot Nixon provided a two-run double on a 3-0 pitch in the third. The pitchers were Derek Lowe (seven innings), Bronson Arroyo (one-third of an inning), Alan Embree (two-thirds of an inning) and Kevin Foulke (one inning). Lowe was the winning pitcher in the final game of all three 2004 postseason series. The final out came when Edgar Renteria hit a comebacker to Foulke, who flipped to Doug Mientkiewicz at first base. The Red Sox were only the fourth team to complete a World Series sweep without trailing in any of the four games, joining the 1963 Dodgers, 1966 Orioles and 1989 Athletics. Three days later, the city of Boston celebrated the title with a huge parade. The Red Sox boarded the eclectic, brightly colored, amphibious "duck boats" and passed a cheering throng (estimated at 3.2 million) that jammed the rain-soaked streets and the banks of the Charles River. On the final leg of the seven-mile parade, the duck boats slid into the water.

**B**

# 28
## October

**T**he question of the day. Who was the second player in World Series history to hit two home runs in a World Series game?

In 1915 Red Sox outfielder Harry Hooper was the second player in World Series history to belt two homers in a game. (Patsy Dougherty was the first.) The Sox won three of the first four games of the Fall Classic against the Phillies and looked to close out the Series in game five on October 13 at Baker Bowl in Philadelphia. Baker Bowl was a bandbox of a ballpark with a capacity of only 18,000. The right-field line was only 272 feet long, the fence in the right center-field power alley was just 300 feet from home plate, and dead center was an even 400 feet. Those cozy dimensions were reduced even further during the 1915 World Series with the addition of temporary seats. In the third inning, with the score 1-1, Hooper bounced a drive into the temporary bleachers in center, which, under the ground rules then in effect, was a home run. The Phillies moved ahead 4-2, but the Sox tied the score 4-4 on a two-run homer by Duffy Lewis into the bleachers. Hooper provided the winning run in the ninth by hitting another homer into the bleachers for a 5-4 victory and the world championship.

# 29
## October

**T**he question of the day.
    What connection does the
    Vendome Hotel in Boston have to
the first World Series in 1903?
    When the 1903 Pittsburgh Pirates
played in the World Series in Boston,
the club stayed at the Vendome Hotel.
More than a century later, it still exists at
the corner of Commonwealth and Dart-
mouth Avenues in the Back Bay. Built in 1871,
it was Boston's most fashionable hotel at the time of baseball's first
World Series and once boasted Presidents Ulysses S. Grant and
Grover Cleveland as guests, in addition to Mark Twain, John D.
Rockefeller, Thomas Edison, P. T. Barnum, Oscar Wilde and Sarah
Bernhardt. In 1882, it became the first commercial building in
Boston to install electric lighting. The Vendome was renovated as
a condominium complex during the 1970s, although with tragic
consequences. A fire broke out during the renovation in June 1972,
and nine Boston firefighters lost their lives combating the blaze.

# 30
## October

**R**ex Cecil, a pitcher with the Red Sox in 1944 and 1945, died on this date in 1966. He had a wild ride to his major league debut on August 13, 1944. Cecil came from the San Diego Padres of the Pacific Coast League. On Friday August 11, he was tossed off a plane in Tucson, Arizona, because of military priorities. After several hours walking the streets in search of lodging, he finally got a flight Saturday afternoon and arrived in Boston on Sunday. The secretary of general manager Eddie Collins met Cecil at the Boston airport and hustled him into a taxicab. When he arrived at Fenway, it was the first time he had ever been in a major league ballpark. With almost no sleep during the previous 48 hours, Cecil made his debut entering a game against the Browns with the score 6-6 and the temperature reading 100 degrees. He pitched four shutout innings and the Red Sox won 7-6 in the 13th. Cecil had little more success in the majors, however. He finished his career with a 6-10 record and a 5.18 ERA.

**B**

# 31
## October

**T**he question of the day.
How did a rat change the
course of television history?

One of the most enduring television images in World Series history took place in the 12th inning of game six in 1975, when Carlton Fisk ended the contest with a home run to give the Red Sox a thrilling 7-6 victory over the Reds. Fisk stopped to watch the flight of the ball while he was positioned a few feet down the first base line and waved his arms in an attempt to use body English to steer the ball into fair territory. After the ball struck the foul pole for a homer, Fisk leaped into the air and circled the bases amid jubilant fans who stormed the field. Television cameras may not have captured Fisk's gyrations if it hadn't been for a large rat inside the Fenway Park scoreboard. Cameraman Lou Gerard was stationed inside the scoreboard with his lens poked through a hole, and his instructions were to follow the flight of the ball. When Fisk made contact with Pat Darcy's pitch, Gerard was distracted by a rat about four feet away from him, and the sight of the rodent froze him long enough to allow him to stay with Fisk and get the famous reaction shot. Since then, reaction shots have been a staple of sports television coverage.

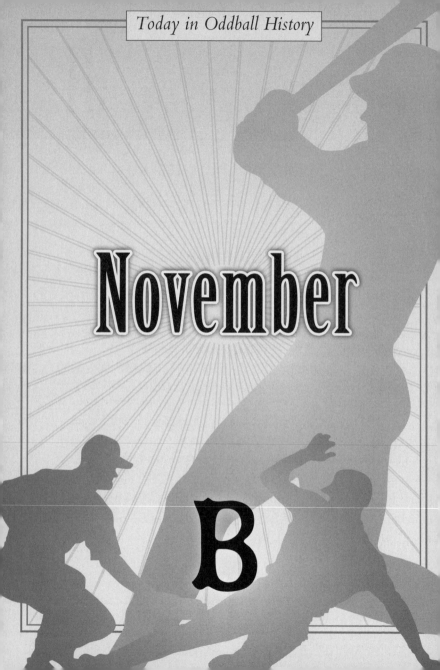

# November

B

**01**
**November**

On this date in 1916, Red Sox owner Joe Lannin sold the franchise to New York theatrical producers Harry Frazee and Hugh Ward. Four years earlier, Frazee had made an unsuccessful bid to purchase the St. Louis Cardinals. In addition to producing plays, Frazee owned theaters in New York and Chicago. He also promoted the Jack Johnson-Jess Willard heavyweight boxing title match in Havana in 1915, which many to this day believe was fixed in Willard's favor. A native of Peoria, Illinois, Frazee was 36 years old when he bought the Sox and offered half the sale amount of $675,000 in cash and planned to pay the balance using loans he would cover with profits from the team. The purchase price included Fenway Park. Ward was a silent partner who was rarely heard from. Frazee led the Red Sox to a world championship in 1918, but he soon dismantled the roster when World War I began, and a losing club cut into his profits about the same time the payment on the loans came due. To help pay his debts, Frazee sold Babe Ruth to the Yankees in January 1920, an act that sealed his notorious legacy in Boston and baseball history. Frazee sold the Red Sox in July 1923 before making millions producing the highly successful play *No, No, Nannette.* He died from Bright's disease in 1929.

**B**

# 02
## November

**H**appy Birthday Greg Harris. A pitcher with the Red Sox from 1989 through 1994, Harris was born on this date in 1955. He was involved in a strange game in New York on September 18, 1993, when the Yankees beat the Red Sox 4-3 with the help of an "extra out." With two out in the ninth inning, the Sox leading 3-1, Harris on the mound, and a Yankee runner on first base, Mike Stanley flied out to Mike Greenwell in left field to apparently end the game. But third base umpire Tim Welke waved off the play because a fan jumped from a box seat and ran onto the field. Given another chance, Stanley singled. Wade Boggs followed with another single to score a run. After Dion James walked, Don Mattingly drove in the tying and winning runs with another single. The Red Sox protested the game but the American League disallowed it. According to many of the Red Sox, the pitch by Harris to Stanley was on the way to the plate before Welke called time. The fan who ran onto the field was a 15-year-old from Pleasantville, New York, who was attending the game with a church group. It wasn't the only bizarre play of the day. In the first inning, Mo Vaughn threw his bat away and trotted to first base believing he had received ball four from Jimmy Key. It was ball three. On the next pitch, Vaughn hit a home run.

**03**
**November**

**T**he question of the day.
Who was Tracy Stallard?
On the final day of the 1961
season, Tracy Stallard and the Red Sox
played a supporting role in baseball
history as Roger Maris broke Babe
Ruth's single-season home run record
with his 61st for the only run of a 1-0
Yankees win in New York. Maris entered
the day tied with Ruth, who hit 60 in 1927. The
homer was struck off Stallard in the fourth inning. Maris was 1-for-4
in the game. Stallard induced Maris to fly to Carl Yastrzemski in
left in the second inning and struck out Maris on a 3-2 pitch in
the sixth. In the eighth against Chet Nichols, Maris popped out to
second baseman Chuck Schilling. Maris held the record until Mark
McGwire hit 70 home runs for the Cardinals in 1998. Stallard had a
lifetime record of 30-57 and was on the wrong end of history again
on June 21, 1964. While pitching for the Mets, Stallard was the losing pitcher when Jim Bunning pitched a perfect game.

**B**

# 04
## November

Jake Powell, an outfielder in the majors from 1930 through 1945, died on this date in 1948 while in police custody in Washington, D.C. Powell pulled a gun and committed suicide after being arrested for allegedly passing bad checks. He was involved in a vicious fight with Red Sox player-manager Joe Cronin while playing for the Yankees on May 30, 1938, before 82,990 at Yankee Stadium, the largest crowd ever to see a Red Sox regular season game. The Yankees won both ends of a double-header 10-0 and 5-4. The trouble started when Powell, who worked as a sheriff's deputy in South Carolina during the off-season, rushed toward Sox pitcher Archie McKain after being hit by a pitch. Before Powell could square off at McKain, Cronin rushed from his shortstop position and took a swing at Powell, who retaliated. Cronin and Powell were ejected by the umpires but started fighting again under the grandstand. In the second melee, Powell clawed Cronin's face.

# 05 November

**T**he question of the day.
How many pro football teams have called Fenway Park home?

The present-day Washington Redskins have their origins in Boston, playing in the NFL for the first time in 1932. The Redskins used Braves Field as a home field in 1932, and Fenway Park from 1933 through 1936. The first NFL game at Fenway took place on October 8, 1933, with the Redskins defeating the New York Giants 21-20 before a crowd of 15,000. The Boston Redskins won the Eastern Division title in 1936, but the crowds were so small during the season that the club moved the NFL championship game against the Green Bay Packers to the Polo Grounds in New York. The Redskins moved to Washington in 1937. Another National Football League team called the Boston Yanks played at Fenway from 1944 through 1948. Meager crowds forced owner Ted Collins to move the club to New York. Through many name changes and relocations, the franchise is now the Indianapolis Colts. The team was known as the New York Bulldogs in 1949, the New York Yanks in 1950 and 1951, the Dallas Texans in 1952 and the Baltimore Colts from 1953 through 1983 before moving to Indianapolis. The Boston Patriots, established in 1960, played at Fenway from 1963 through 1968. The team was renamed the New England Patriots in 1971.

# 06
## November

**O**n this date in 1976, the Red Sox signed Bill Campbell, most recently with the Twins, as a free agent. Campbell was the first free agent to sign with any major league club after the system went into effect at the end of the 1976 season. He was the losing pitcher in the first two games of the 1977 season, but finished the year with a 13-9 record, 31 saves and a 2.96 ERA. With starters struggling for consistency, Campbell's 13 wins led the club. He pitched 140 innings of relief in 1977 after throwing an average of 136 innings in his last three years in Minnesota. An elbow injury in 1978, which was probably the result of overwork, ended Campball's days as a closer, although he remained in the majors until 1987. He pitched for the Sox until 1982, when he was traded to the Cubs.

**07**
**November**

**T**he question of the day.
What is the only team to hit three home runs in an inning in a World Series game?

The 1967 Red Sox are the only team to hit three homers in an inning during the World Series. On October 11, the Sox were playing the Cardinals at Fenway Park when in game six, Carl Yastrzemski led off the fourth inning with a homer off Dick Hughes. After the next two hitters were retired, Reggie Smith and Rico Petrocelli hit back-to-back home runs off Hughes. Petrocelli also homered in the second. The four homers produced only four runs, however, and the Sox needed four more runs in the seventh to break a 4-4 tie. Joe Foy's double broke the deadlock. The winning pitcher was Gary Waslewski, who went 5⅓ innings. Waslewski was in his first major league season and had started only eight games in his career and possessed just two big-league victories.

**B**

# 08
## November

**T**he question of the day.
Who is the youngest pitcher in World Series history?

Ken Brett is the youngest pitcher to appear in the World Series. Brett was less than a month past his 19th birthday and had pitched in only one big-league game when he was called upon to pitch the eighth inning of game four for the Red Sox on October 8, 1967, against the Cardinals in St. Louis. Brett contributed a scoreless inning, but the Red Sox lost 6-0. He also pitched one-third of an inning in game seven. Brett played 14 seasons in the majors and spent time with 10 clubs. Following his term with the Red Sox, Brett played for the Brewers, Phillies, Pirates, Yankees, White Sox, Angels, Twins and Dodgers before finishing his career as a teammate of his brother George in Kansas City. After his big-league career was over, Brett did a Miller Lite commercial in which he couldn't figure out what town he was in.

## 09
### November

**T**he question of the day.

How was Carl Yastrzemski honored at Fenway Park when he retired in 1983?

In celebration of his 23-year major league career, Carl Yastrzemski was honored in pregame festivities on October 1. When he walked out of the dugout to second base, where microphones were placed, he received a six-minute standing ovation. During the ceremony, a letter from President Ronald Reagan was read, and Governor Michael Dukakis and Senator Edward Kennedy were there. The ceremony ended with Yastrzemski taking a dramatic and emotional trot around the perimeter of the playing field, shaking hands with as many fans as possible and waving to the crowd of 33,491. Yaz was hitless in four at-bats, including the final out, in a 3-1 loss to the Indians. After the game, he repeated his lap around the field, shaking more hands. The following day, Yastrzemski played in his final game, a 3-1 win over the Indians at Fenway. He was listed in the starting lineup in left field, a position he hadn't played since 1980. Yaz collected a single in three at-bats before leaving in the seventh inning to a standing ovation. After the game, he circled the field to shake hands as he had the previous day, then spent an hour signing autographs outside the ballpark.

**B**

# 10
## November

**T**he question of the day.

What is the most number of runs scored by a team in a post-season game?

During the 1999 American Division Series, the Red Sox fell behind the Indians two games to none, then won three in a row by scores of 9-3, 23-7 at Fenway Park and 12-8 in Cleveland to advance to the Championship Series. The 23 runs in game four is the most ever scored by a team in a postseason game. The Sox also set postseason records for hits (24) and margin of victory (16). John Valentin had two homers, a double and a single and drove in seven runs. Jose Offerman and Jason Varitek also homered for the Sox. Varitek set a postseason record with five runs scored. He also drove in three runs and had two doubles and a single in addition to his homer. Offerman drove in five runs and scored three. Mike Stanley garnered five hits, including a triple, in six at-bats. The five hits tied a postseason record. Trot Nixon drove in five runs and scored three, and Darren Lewis crossed the plate three times. The Sox scored two runs in the first inning, five in the second, three in the third, five in the fourth, three in the fifth, three in the seventh and two in the eighth.

**B**

# 11
## November

**T**he question of the day. What two plays involving Chuck Knoblauch and Jose Offerman altered the course of the 1999 American League Championship Series?

The Yankees beat the Red Sox four games to one in the 1999 ALCS with the help of a couple of controversial plays. In the top of the 10th of game one on October 13, with the score tied 3-3, umpire Rick Reed ruled that Yankee second baseman Chuck Knoblauch held onto a throw from third baseman Scott Brosius long enough to record a force out of Jose Offerman. However, replays showed that Knoblauch never had full control and that Offerman should have been ruled safe. In the bottom half, Bernie Williams hit a walk-off homer for a 4-3 Yankee win. Reed later admitted he blew the call. There was another controversial play involving Knoblauch and Offerman in game four, a 9-2 Yankees win at Fenway Park on October 17. With the Yankees ahead 3-2 in the bottom of the eighth, Knoblauch fumbled a hard-hit grounder and tried to tag Offerman running from first base to second. Knoblauch missed the tag and threw wide of second in an attempt to force the runner, but umpire Tim Tschida called Offerman out. Tschida later admitted he made the wrong call.

# 12
# November

**H**appy Birthday Carl Mays. A pitcher with the Red Sox from 1915 through 1919 and in the majors from 1915 through 1929, Carl Mays was born on this date in 1891. Controversy seemed to follow him throughout his career. A case in point was a 6-1 win over the Senators in Washington on June 30, 1916. In the third inning, Mays hit George McBride with a pitch. McBride responded by throwing his bat at Mays. Both benches emptied, and in the ensuing brawl, Red Sox catcher Sam Agnew was arrested and hauled off to jail, where he was booked on assault charges for punching Senators manager Clark Griffith in the face. Mays swore out a warrant for McBride's arrest. It wasn't the only bizarre incident of the afternoon. In the seventh inning, Clyde Milan of the Senators fouled back a pitch that struck umpire Brick Owens in the throat. Owens swallowed the chewing tobacco he had in his cheek and nearly choked to death. It took 15 minutes for Owens to regain his faculties and continue the game. The following day in a Washington courtroom, Agnew was acquitted when Griffith refused to press charges, but Agnew was fined $10 for disorderly conduct. McBride was also exonerated when Mays withdrew his request for a warrant.

**13**
**November**

**T**he question of the day.
Was there ever an all-Boston World Series?

Boston had two major league teams from 1901 through 1952. During that period, the Red Sox won the American League pennant in 1903, 1904, 1912, 1915, 1916, 1918 and 1946. The Braves took the National League crown in 1914 and 1948. There was never an all-Boston World Series, but it nearly happened in 1948. The Red Sox and Indians ended the regular season in a tie with identical records of 96-58 before the Indians won a one-game playoff 8-3 at Fenway Park. The Indians beat the Braves in the World Series four games to two. The 1948 season was the only one in which both Boston teams were in first place simultaneously after September 1.

# 14
## November

**T**he question of the day.
Who was Al Luplow?
Al Luplow was an outfielder
who played in the majors from 1961
through 1967. While a member of
the Indians on June 27, 1963, he made
what is arguably the greatest catch in
Fenway Park history in the eighth inning
of a 6-4 Red Sox loss. With two Boston runners on base, Dick Williams hit a drive to right.
Running at full speed, Luplow headed toward the five-foot-high
barrier that fronted the bullpen. He reached over the fence and
backhanded the ball just as his knees hit the wall. Luplow flipped
over the fence head-first and hung on for the out.

**B**

**15
November**

**T**he question of the day.
Who was Ellis Kinder?
Ellis Kinder pitched for the
Red Sox from 1948 through 1955
during an unusual career. The son of an
Arkansas sharecropper, Kinder didn't
make his professional debut until he was
24 years old and didn't reach the majors
with the St. Louis Browns until he was 31,
earning him the nickname "Old Folks." Heading
into the 1949 season, Kinder was 34 and had a lifetime record of
21-25. That year he broke out with a 23-6 record and a 3.36 ERA.
After a 14-12 mark in 1950, Kinder was converted into a reliever.
In 1951, he was 11-2 with 14 saves and a 2.55 ERA in 69 games and
127 innings. Kinder was even better at the age of 38 in 1953, when
he had a 10-6 record, 27 saves and an earned run average of 1.85.
The only other Red Sox pitcher with a 20-win season and a 20-save
season is Derek Lowe.

**B**

# 16
## November

**T**he question of the day.
Who was Billy Jurges?
Billy Jurges managed the Red Sox from July 1959 through June 1960 to a record of 59-63. He was replaced as manager on an interim basis by Del Baker, a 68-year-old coach, for an "indefinite period." The Red Sox had a record of 18-31 when Jurges was relieved of his duties. Ill health was cited as the reason. Dr. Richard Wright, a Boston internal medicine specialist, examined Jurges and said the Red Sox skipper was "completely exhausted from a fruitless task." The fruitless task was trying to turn an untalented Red Sox team into a winner. Jurges went home to Silver Springs, Maryland, and composed a letter to team owner Tom Yawkey stating the conditions under which he would return as manager. The letter was sent by airmail special delivery. After receiving the letter, Yawkey sent Jurges a reply by airmail special delivery informing him he had been fired.

**B**

# 17
## November

On this date in 1947, the Red Sox traded Roy Partee, Jim Wilson, Al Widmar, Eddie Pellagrini, Pete Layden, Joe Ostrowski and $310,000 to the Browns for Vern Stephens and Jack Kramer. The two clubs weren't done dealing. A day later, the Red Sox sent Sam Dente, Clem Dreisewerd, Bill Sommers and $65,000 to St. Louis for Ellis Kinder and Bill Hitchcock. Arguably the most underrated player of his generation, and possibly in baseball history, Stephens became Boston's starting shortstop while Johnny Pesky moved to third base. Displaying rare power for a man of his position, Stephens hit .285 with 98 home runs and 440 RBIs in 459 games in his first three seasons with the Red Sox. He accounted for 29 home runs in 1948, 39 in 1949 and 30 in 1950. His runs-batted-in totals those three years were 137, 159 and 144. No one in major league baseball has driven in as many as 440 runs in three consecutive seasons since 1940. Sammy Sosa came closest with 439 from 1999 through 2001. Stephens made eight All-Star teams and ranked in the top 10 in the MVP voting six times. Despite his accomplishments over a 15-year career and favorable statistics, he never made it to the Hall of Fame.

# 18
## November

**O**n this date in 1997, the Red Sox traded Carl Pavano and Tony Armas, Jr. to the Expos for Pedro Martinez. At the time of the trade, Martinez was 26 years old and signed only through 1998, but the Red Sox locked him up for six years and $75 million. It was a huge gamble. Prior to 1997, Martinez was a solid but unspectacular pitcher with a 48-31 record and a 3.39 ERA. In 1997, he broke loose with a 17-8 record and a league-leading 1.90 ERA and 3-05 strikeouts in 241⅓ innings in winning the Cy Young Award. Martinez proved to be worth the investment as he had only scratched the surface of his potential in Montreal. In seven seasons with the Red Sox, he had a record of 117-37 and an ERA of 2.52 along with 1,649 strikeouts in 1,383⅔ innings. His .760 winning percentage during his seven years with the Sox has been exceeded by only one other pitcher over seven consecutive seasons (minimum 75 decisions). The only other hurler to post a better mark was Lefty Grove, whose winning percentage was .776 (160-40) from 1928 through 1934. Among Red Sox pitchers, Martinez ranks first in winning percentage, sixth in wins, third in strikeouts and sixth in ERA (minimum 1,000 innings).

**B**

**19**
November

**T**he question of the day.
     What strange convergence of events happened on August 31, 2004?

    On that date, 16-year-old Lee Gavin was hit in the face by a Manny Ramirez foul ball during a 10-7 win over the Angels at Fenway Park. Gavin lost two teeth in the accident. He lived at 558 Dutton Road in suburban Sudbury in the very house where Babe Ruth resided from 1916 through 1926. The Red Sox hoped that the connection was an indication that the Curse of the Bambino had been lifted. Stranger still, that same night, the Yankees lost 22-0 to the Indians in the most lopsided shutout in modern major league history. Less than two months later, the Sox overcame a three-games-to-none deficit in the American League Championship Series to beat the Yankees, then swept the Cardinals in the World Series.

# 20
## November

**O**n this date in 1962, the Red Sox traded Jim Pagliaroni and Don Schwall to the Pirates for Dick Stuart and Jack Lamabe. Cocky and controversial, Stuart both thrilled and exasperated fans in two seasons with the Red Sox with his big bat, big mouth and iron glove. He hit 75 homers and drove in 232 runs in 1963 and 1964, but he earned the nickname "Dr. Strangeglove" with his atrocious fielding. Stuart, it seemed, cared little about anyone but himself. "I'm not going to get famous hitting singles or fielding ground balls," Stuart said. He was wrong. His fielding, or lack of it, was the stuff of legend. In two seasons in Boston, Stuart made 53 errors, more than any other two AL first basemen put together. He led the league in errors seven straight seasons beginning in 1958. Stuart could be likable when the mood struck him, and his outrageous behavior made him popular with fans. He even had his own television program on WBZ, called *Stuart on Sports,* which was on every Sunday night. He signed for the show before he played a single game for the Sox. But Stuart was not a team player, and his selfishness undermined manager Johnny Pesky's efforts to change the team attitude. After two years, the Red Sox shipped him to the Phillies.

**21
November**

**T**he question of the day.
Who was the last American League pitcher to hit two home runs in a game?

Red Sox pitcher Sonny Siebert was the last American League pitcher to hit two homers in a game before the designated hitter rule was adopted in 1973. He accomplished the feat on September 2, 1971, by driving in all three Boston runs and pitching a shutout to defeat the Orioles 3-0 at Fenway Park. Siebert hit a solo homer in the third inning and a two-run shot on the fifth, both off Pat Dobson. Siebert hit six home runs in 1971 and batted .266 in 79 at-bats. Other Red Sox pitchers with five or more homers in a season are Wes Ferrell (seven in 1935 and five in 1936) and Earl Wilson (five in 1964 and six in 1965). Before entering professional baseball, Siebert was a star basketball player at the University of Missouri and was selected by the St. Louis Hawks in the NBA draft.

# 22
## November

One of the worst days in American history took place on this date in 1963 when President John Kennedy was assassinated in Dallas. The Red Sox honored Kennedy with ceremonies on Opening Day, April 17, 1964, before 20,213 at Fenway Park. The home team won 4-1 over the White Sox. The proceeds of the game went to Kennedy's presidential library fund. His brother Robert, then attorney general, threw out the first pitch. Others in attendance included Senator Edward Kennedy, sisters Jean Smith and Patricia Lawford, Massachusetts Governor Endicott Peabody, Mayor John Collins, Stan Musial, then head of the national physical fitness program, stage star Carol Channing, TV comedian Frank Fontaine, and former boxing champions Jack Dempsey and Gene Tunney. The gate receipts totaled $36,818. The library opened on Columbia Point in 1979 after plans to build it in Cambridge failed to materialize.

B

# 23
## November

**O**n this date in 1977, the Red Sox signed Mike Torrez as a free agent. He won 16 games for the Sox in both 1978 and 1979, but will be long-remembered for the one he didn't win on October 2, 1978, in the one-game playoff against the Yankees to determine the AL East champ. Torrez gave up the infamous three-run homer to Bucky Dent in the seventh inning, which pushed the Yankees to a 5-4 win at Fenway Park. The Sox led 2-0 at the end of the six. Torrez cruised along with six shutout innings until the fateful seventh. Chris Chambliss and Roy White led off the inning with singles. After retiring the next two batters, Torrez faced Dent, who fouled a pitch off his foot on an 0-2 count, causing a delay as the Yankee trainer examined the Yankee shortstop. Dent also cracked his bat and had to retrieve a new one. Torrez stood on the mound growing cold instead of tossing a few warm-up pitches. On his first pitch after play resumed, Dent hit a fly ball to left. In most major league parks, it would have been a warning-track fly ball, at worst. At Fenway it was a three-run homer. The Yankees added another run in the seventh and one in the eighth for a 5-2 lead before the Sox scored two in the bottom of the eighth. Two were on base when Carl Yastrzemski popped out facing Goose Gossage to end the game.

# 24
## November

**T**he question of the day.
What happened on State of Maine Day at Fenway Park in 1958?

On State of Maine Day at Fenway on August 24, 1958, the Red Sox beat the Kansas City Athletics 14-3 in the first game of a double-header and 3-2 in 11 innings in the second tilt. Maine residents came bearing gifts. First baseman Dick Gernert was given a bear cub named Homer, which he later donated to the Birmingham, Alabama, zoo. Outfielder Jackie Jensen was presented with a barrel of lobsters, had them cooked during the second game, and provided them to his teammates after he drove in the winning run with a single.

**B**

**25**
**November**

On this date in 2002, the Red Sox hired Theo Epstein as general manager, replacing Dan Duquette, who was fired. Epstein was not the team's first choice, but at 28, Epstein became the youngest general manager in major league history. He had been the director of baseball operations with the Padres from 2000 through 2002, and the Red Sox hired him in March 2002 as assistant general manager. Epstein grew up in Brookline, about a mile from Fenway Park, as a diehard Red Sox fan. He was a 12-year-old in the family room on October 25, 1986, during game six against the Mets when the Sox were on the brink of winning the World Series for the first time since 1918. "I was watching the game with my brother," he said. "We wanted to be off the ground, if possible in midair, when the ball went into the glove for the last out, so we got on top of the couch to jump. We were standing on top of the couch for about half an hour. It was painful." The hiring of someone so young was a leap of faith for Red Sox owners, but with Epstein's help, Red Sox fans reveled in a world championship in 2004. Epstein dismantled much of that veteran team, and with a younger roster, the Red Sox won another World Series in 2007.

# 26
## November

**T**he question of the day.
When did the Red Sox and Indians combine for a record 19 runs in an inning?

The Red Sox and Indians combined for 19 runs in the eighth inning at Fenway Park in a game won by Cleveland 19-9 on April 7, 1977. The 19 runs by two clubs in one inning is a major league record. The game was routine through seven innings with the score 3-3 before the Indians erupted by 13 runs off Bill Campbell, Jim Willoughby, Tom House and Tom Murphy. The Red Sox countered with six runs in their half of the eighth before the Indians added three in the ninth. The 19 eighth-inning runs scored on a triple, five doubles, eight singles, six walks and an error, but no home runs.

**B**

**27**
**November**

**T**he question of the day.
Who is the only major leaguer to begin his career with six consecutive hits?

Ted Cox, a 22-year-old rookie with the Red Sox in 1977, set a major league record by starting his career with six straight hits. He made his debut on September 18 against the Orioles in Baltimore batting second as the designated hitter. Cox singled in his first at-bat against Mike Flanagan, and after a walk, hit two more singles and a double in the 10-4 Boston win. Cox is the only player in Red Sox history to collect four hits in his first major league game. In his second game on September 19, Cox singled in his first two plate appearances during a 6-3 win over the Yankees at Fenway Park. He played 13 games for the Sox in 1977 and hit .362. The club traded Cox to the Indians before the start of the 1978 season. Despite the fast start, Cox lasted only five years in the majors and finished his career with a .245 batting average and 10 home runs in 272 games.

**B**

# 28
## November

**O**n this date in 2003, the Red Sox traded Casey Fossum, Brandon Lyon, Jorge DeRosa and Michael Goss to the Diamondbacks for Curt Schilling. Schilling returned to the Red Sox after a 15-year absence. The Sox drafted him in 1986, but traded him to the Orioles two years later. In exchange for four marginal prospects, Schilling gave the Red Sox a 21-6 record in 2004, leading the AL in wins and winning percentage while posting a 3.26 ERA. Schilling was also an inspiration in the postseason by overcoming a severe ankle injury— a dislocated tendon—to win three games. Surgery was necessary to completely heal the tendon, but an operation would have put Schilling out for the rest of the season. As a temporary measure, the Red Sox' medical staff sutured the tendon together before each of Schilling's remaining postseason starts. He also wore a specially made shoe that was a half size larger and contained extra foam padding. Blood seeped through to Schilling's sock and became an enduring symbol of the club's world championship season. He is 6-1 with the Red Sox in the postseason. Overall, counting his years with the Phillies and Diamondbacks, Schilling has a 10-2 record and a 2.23 ERA in postseason play.

**29**
**November**

On this date in 1964, the Red Sox traded Dick Stuart to the Phillies for Dennis Bennett. The Sox merely traded one self-centered head case for another. Bennett had only 30 big-league wins when he was acquired by the Sox. Handicapped by a sore shoulder, he was just 12-13 for Boston over three seasons from 1965 through 1967, lived in an apartment over the Playboy Club and frightened teammates by carrying around a suitcase full of handguns. During spring training in Scottsdale in 1965, Bennett fired a half dozen rounds from two pistols at the door of the team's hotel. On another occasion, roommate Lee Thomas asked him to turn out the lights. Bennett did so by shooting the light bulb with a gun. Later, he shot six rounds over the head of sportswriter Will McDonough with a .38 after objecting to one of McDonough's stories. Bennett's daredevil activities also hampered his growth as a pitcher. He participated in bareback bronco events on the rodeo circuit and was a forest firefighter in California.

**B**

# 30
## November

**T**he question of the day.
How did Red Sox fan Paul Giorgio try to reverse the "Curse of the Bambino."

On the advice of a Tibetan Buddhist holy man on May 23, 2001, 37-year-old Paul Giorgio placed a Red Sox cap next to the chorten, a stone altar at the base of Mount Everest where each climbing team burns juniper branches as an offering to the gods. Then he carried the cap to the summit and placed it at 29,028 feet, along with an American flag, to reverse the curse. When he returned to the base camp, Giorgio, as directed by the lama, burned a Yankees cap. A year later, a group of fans made their own attempt to reverse the curse by searching for Babe Ruth's piano at the bottom of Willis Pond in Sudbury, Massachusetts. The pond is adjacent to the house in which Ruth lived from 1916 through 1926. According to local legend, Ruth once threw the upright piano into the water in a drunken rage. The piano was never found.

**B**

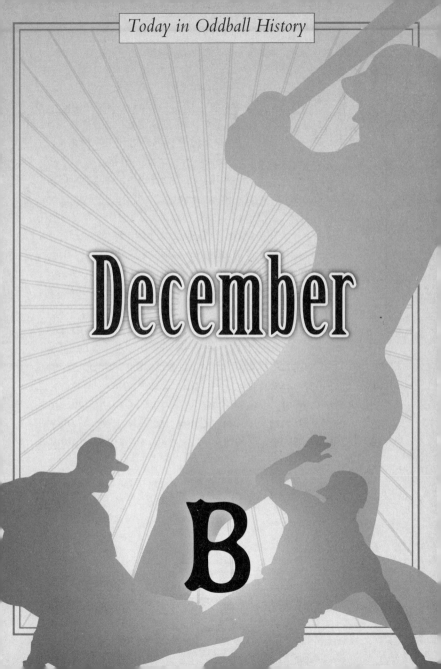

# December

B

# 01
## December

**T**he question of the day.
Which players are in the Red Sox Hall of Fame?

In order to be eligible for the Boston Red Sox Hall of Fame, a player must have played three seasons with the Red Sox and have been retired for three years. Instituted in 1995, the Boston Red Sox Hall of Fame includes the following players, through the 2008 season: Wade Boggs, Rick Burleson, Jimmy Collins, Tony Conigliaro, Joe Cronin, Dom DiMaggio, Bobby Doerr, Dennis Eckersley, Dwight Evans, Rick Ferrell, Wes Ferrell, Boo Ferriss, Carlton Fisk, Jimmie Foxx, Larry Gardner, Billy Goodman, Mike Greenwell, Lefty Grove, Harry Hooper, Tex Hughson, Bruce Hurst, Jackie Jensen, Ellis Kinder, Bill Lee, Duffy Lewis, Jim Lonborg, Fred Lynn, Frank Malzone, Bill Monbouquette, Mel Parnell, Johnny Pesky, Rico Petrocelli, Dick Radatz, Jim Rice, Pete Runnels, Babe Ruth, Everett Scott, George Scott, Reggie Smith, Vern Stephens, Tris Speaker, Bob Stanley, Luis Tiant, Mo Vaughn, Ted Williams, Smoky Joe Wood, Carl Yastrzemski and Cy Young.

**02**
December

**T**he question of the day. Who is the best retired player who has *not* been elected to the Boston Red Sox Hall of Fame?

Among those eligible, the best player *not* in the Red Sox Hall of Fame is Freddie Parent, a shortstop with the club from 1901 through 1907. The Sox won six AL pennants and five world championships from 1903 through 1918, but players from that era are underrepresented in the club's Hall of Fame. Others who merit consideration are second baseman Hobe Ferris (1901–07), outfielder Chick Stahl (1901–06), pitcher Bill Dinneen (1902–07), pitcher George Winter (1901–08), pitcher Jesse Tannehill (1904–08), pitcher Ray Collins (1909–15), shortstop Heinie Wagner (1906–16), and pitcher Carl Mays (1915–19). Others who should be considered are outfielder Ira Flagstead (1923–29), catcher Sammy White (1951–59), outfielder Jimmy Piersall (1952–58), pitcher Frank Sullivan (1953–60), pitcher Tom Brewer (1954-61), shortstop Eddie Bressoud (1962–64), second baseman Mike Andrews (1966–70), catcher Rich Gedman (1980–90), second baseman Marty Barrett (1982–90), outfielder Ellis Burks (1987–92; 2004) and infielder John Valentin (1992–2001).

# 03
## December

**T**he question of the day.
What changes were made to Fenway Park between the 1975 and 1976 seasons?

An electronic scoreboard with video replay capability was added above the center-field bleachers. To support advertising panels, sheet metal was added to the wall above the bleachers. They were the first commercial advertisements inside the ballpark since 1946. The left-field wall was also rebuilt. Before 1976, the wall was composed of wooden railroad ties covered with tin and set atop a concrete base. The old tin panels were replaced by a Formica-type covering that yielded more consistent caroms and less noise. Padding was also added to the wall to protect outfielders. The National League portion of the scoreboard was removed, and the remaining portion of the board was recentered by shifting it to the right. The tin panels were cut into small squares and sold, with the proceeds going to the Jimmy Fund, which supported cancer research.

# 04
## December

**O**n this date in 2003, the Red Sox hired Terry Francona as manager. Red Sox fans didn't greet the announcement warmly. Francona had previously managed the Phillies to a 285-333 record, a less than stellar .440 winning percentage, from 1997 through 2000. He was a coach with the Rangers in 2002 and the Athletics in 2003. From 1981 through 1990, Francona was a light-hitting first baseman with the Expos, Reds, Indians and Brewers. His father, Tito, had played in the majors with nine clubs between 1956 and 1970.

Terry silenced his critics by guiding the Red Sox to their first world championship in 86 years. In the ALCS against the Yankees, the Sox became the first team in baseball history to overcome a three-games-to-none deficit to win a postseason series, then swept the Cardinals in the World Series. The Sox won the World Series again with a sweep of the Rockies in 2007. Francona is only the second manager in Red Sox history to win two world championships, matching Bill Carrigan, who accomplished the feat in 1915 and 1916. Francona is also the first manager in major league history to win his first eight World Series games.

**B**

# 05
## December

**H**appy Birthday Boo Ferriss
A pitcher with the Red Sox from 1945 through 1950, Boo Ferriss was born on this date in 1921. He burst onto the scene as a rookie in 1945 with a record of 21-10, then followed up with a 25-6 mark in 1946. Ferriss developed arm trouble, however, and won only 19 more games after 1946, finishing his career with 65 wins and 30 losses. Ferriss was the talk of baseball with his spectacular start in 1945. Attendance increased by the thousands every time he pitched. Ferriss's only previous professional experience was a 7-7 record with Greensboro in the Piedmont League in 1942. In college, Ferriss was a left-handed outfielder until his arm went bad. Fortunately, Ferriss was ambidextrous and was able to convert to right-handed pitching. Ferriss was given a discharge from the Army Air Corps in February 1945 because of asthma, but wasn't expected to provide much help to the Sox. Manager Joe Cronin turned to him after the club lost their first eight games, however, and Ferriss responded by winning his first eight starts, each of them complete games, including shutouts in his first two starts. His accomplishment of 22 shutout innings at the start of his career was an American League record until Brad Ziegler of the Athletics passed him in 2008.

**06**
**December**

**O**n this date in 1976, the Red Sox traded Cecil Cooper to the Brewers for George Scott and Bernie Carbo. The trade brought Scott back to Boston after five seasons in Milwaukee. Scott hit 33 homers for the Sox in 1977 before weight problems caught up with him and reduced him to a reserve role. Ironically, the Sox traded Scott to the Brewers in October 1971, because they believed that Cooper was ready to take over at first base. When Cooper failed to develop to the satisfaction of Red Sox management, the club dealt him to Milwaukee to get Scott back. It proved to be a huge mistake. While Scott had one good season in his return to New England, Cooper had seven great seasons with the Brewers. From 1977 through 1983, Cooper hit .300 or better each season, and .316 overall, along with an average of 22 homers and 95 RBIs per season. Like Scott, Carbo went from the Red Sox to the Brewers and back again. He played for the Sox at least part of every season from 1974 through 1978. Carbo was little more than a platoon outfielder or designated hitter, but his offbeat sense of humor, Italian ancestry and two pinch-hit home runs in the 1975 World Series made him a popular figure among Boston fans.

# 07
## December

**T**he question of the day.
What was the first American League team to use an airplane to travel from one city to another?

On July 30, 1936, the Red Sox became the first American League team and the second in the majors to travel by airplane. The flight on American Airlines from St. Louis to Chicago took 90 minutes. Five players refused to fly and instead took the train. The next day, the Red Sox defeated the White Sox 7-3. The first major league team to fly was the Cincinnati Reds in 1934. The Reds traveled in three planes, however. The Red Sox were the first big-league club to board a single airplane. Plane travel wasn't common until the 1950s when jet planes were introduced.

**08**
**December**

**H**appy Birthday Jim Pagliaroni
Jim Pagliaroni was born on
this date in 1937. He became the
youngest player in Red Sox history on
August 13, 1955, when he made his
major league debut at the age of 17
years, 248 days during an 18-9 loss to
the Senators at Fenway Park. He entered
the game as a substitute catcher for Sammy
White and hit a sacrifice fly in his only plate
appearance. Pagliaroni was on the team because of a rule passed
in 1955 stipulating that any amateur player who signed a contract
with a bonus of at least $4,000 would have to remain on the roster
for two years. The rule was rescinded in 1958. The Red Sox gave
him $70,000 to sign just after he graduated from high school. Pagli-
aroni didn't play another major league game until 1960. He went
into the Army after the 1955 season ended, and after his discharge,
spent three seasons in the minors. Pagliaroni was the Red Sox starting catcher in 1961 and 1962 before being traded to the Pirates.
The youngest player to hit a home run for the Sox is Gerry Moses
on May 25, 1965, at 18 years and 289 days. It came off Mudcat
Grant during a 17-5 loss to the Twins at Fenway Park and was Moses' first major league hit. A catcher, Moses didn't collect his second
hit and second homer until September 15, 1968. He finished his
big-league career in 1975 with 25 homers.

**B**

# 09
## December

**T**he question of the day.
Who is the youngest pitcher in Red Sox history?

The youngest pitcher in Red Sox history is Chuck Stobbs, who made his debut on September 15, 1947, at 18 years, 75 days. He is also the youngest player of any kind to start a game. Smoky Joe Wood is the youngest pitcher to win a game and pitch a shutout—both occurring in a 6-0 win over the Indians in Boston on September 16, 1911—when he was 18 years, 326 days. The last teenager to play for the Red Sox was Luis Alvarado at 19 in 1968.

**B**

# 10
### December

**O**n this date in 1935, the Red Sox sent Gordon Rhoades, George Saviano and $100,000 to the Athletics for Jimmie Foxx and Johnny Marcum. One of the best first basemen ever to don a uniform (many baseball historians rank him second only to Lou Gehrig), Foxx was a little past his peak but gave the Red Sox six terrific seasons, particularly in 1938, when he hit 50 homers. It stood as the club record until David Ortiz had 54 in 2006. Foxx still holds the club record for RBIs in a season with 175 in 1938.

# 11
# December

**T**he question of the day. Who is the oldest player in Red Sox history?

The oldest player in Red Sox history is Deacon McGuire, who was manager of the club in 1908 and put himself into one game as a pinch-hitter at the age of 44 and was 0-for-1. The oldest player to start a game is Carl Yastrzemski at 44 years, 41 days on October 2, 1983, in his last appearance. Yaz collected a single in three at-bats during a 3-1 win over the Indians at Fenway Park. He is also the oldest with a home run, struck on September 10, 1983, during an 8-6 loss to the Indians in Cleveland. Rickey Henderson, at 43 in 2002, is the oldest Red Sox player with a triple and a stolen base. The oldest pitcher is Dennis Eckersley, who was eight days shy of his 44th birthday when he made his last big-league appearance as a member of the Red Sox during a 9-6 win over the Orioles at Fenway Park on September 24, 1998. Seven days earlier, Eckersley became the oldest Red Sox hurler with a victory. David Wells is the oldest starting pitcher at 43 years, 98 days on August 26, 2006. Cy Young is the oldest with a shutout at 41 in 1908. Mike Ryba is the oldest Red Sox player to participate in a World Series game. A relief pitcher, Ryba was 43 in 1946. He played 10 seasons in the majors, the first in 1935 when he was 32.

**12**
**December**

On this date in 1933, the Red Sox traded Bob Kline and Rabbit Warster, along with $160,000, to the Athletics for Lefty Grove, Rube Walberg and Max Bishop. After winning the American League pennant for three consecutive seasons between 1929 and 1931, Connie Mack found he couldn't pay his aging stars in a Depression economy. He was $200,000 in debt, and for the second time in his career, Mack was in the process of dismantling a championship team. With Tom Yawkey's millions behind them, the Red Sox were well positioned. Grove was the best pitcher in baseball in 1933. From 1927 through 1933, he compiled an amazing 172-54 record for Philadelphia. His career total against the Red Sox was 35-8. Grove was 34 years old when he pitched his first game with the Sox, and was no longer in top form, but he still went 105-62 in eight seasons in Boston. He also led the league in ERA for four seasons with the Sox to give him a record nine ERA titles for his career. Plagued from the outset of spring training by a sore arm, Grove was 8-8 with a 6.50 ERA in 1934. Walberg and Bishop were also key members of the Athletics 1929-31 championship teams, but neither was much help to the Red Sox.

# 13

## December

**O**n this date in 1996, Roger Clemens signed with the Blue Jays as a free agent. The Red Sox lost one of the best pitchers in baseball history. Clemens wanted a four-year contract and publicly stated that he hoped to end his career in Boston. The Red Sox were in a tough position determining whether 34-year-old Clemens was worth a mega-million, four-year deal that would keep him among the highest-paid players in baseball. In the end, general manager Dan Duquette believed Clemens was in "the twilight of his career" and not worth a long-term deal. The Blue Jays and several other clubs involved in the bidding war for Clemens didn't share Duquette's reservations. To the Red Sox everlasting regret, Clemens signed with Toronto for $24.75 million over three years, the most money ever paid to a pitcher up to that point. Clemens returned to his former glory. From 1997 through 2007, Clemens won four Cy Young Awards with three different clubs. His record was 162-73.

B

**14**
**December**

**T**he question of the day.
What is the only club to post winning percentages of .600 or better three consecutive seasons without reaching the World Series?

The Red Sox from 1948 through 1950 are the only club with winning percentages of .600 three years in a row without a World Series appearance. The Sox were 96-59 (.619) in 1948, 96-58 (.623) in 1949 and 94-60 (.610) in 1950. With Joe McCarthy as manager, the Red Sox lost the pennant on the final day in 1948 to the Yankees and again by a single game in 1949 to the Yankees. McCarthy was replaced as manager in June 1950 by Steve O'Neill, and the Sox finished four games behind the Yankees. It is part of the curious legacy of Joe McCarthy that he never won a close pennant race. He won nine league titles—one with the Cubs and eight with the Yankees—and the smallest margin over the second-place club in those nine seasons was nine games. Yet he lost five pennants by three games or less. Those five were with the Cubs in 1930 (two games), Yankees in 1935 (three games) and 1940 (two games) and the Red Sox in 1948 (one game) and in 1949 (one game). With a few breaks, the Red Sox of 1946–50 could have won four AL pennants and created a dynasty.

# 15
## December

**T**he question of the day.
What was the Red Sox record at Fenway Park from 1946 through 1952?

Part of the reason for the failure of the Red Sox to reach the World Series more than once from 1946 through 1952 was the fact that the roster was constructed with the cozy dimensions of Fenway Park in mind. During those seven seasons, the Sox were nearly unbeatable at home, with a record of 381-158 for a winning percentage of .707. Road games were another story. The Red Sox were 255-284, a winning percentage of .473. The Red Sox led the AL in home winning percentage in 1946, 1948, 1949, 1950, 1952 and 1958.

# 16
## December

The question of the day.

What is the only time during the last 40 years that the Red Sox have experienced three losing seasons in a row?

The only time since 1966 in which the Red Sox have had three losing seasons were in 1992 (73-89), 1993 (80-82) and the strike-shortened season of 1994 (54-61). Butch Hobson was the manager all three seasons. A former football star at the University of Alabama, Hobson was a hustling third baseman for the Red Sox from 1975 through 1980, then managed the club's top farm team in Pawtucket. The front office loved his personal toughness, which drew comparisons to Dick Williams. Hobson was overmatched as a manager at the major league level, however. He was later arrested for cocaine possession while a manager at Wilkes-Barre in the Phillies system. Since 2000, Hobson has been a manager in the independent leagues.

**B**

# 17
## December

**T**he question of the day.

What is the earliest date for a regular-season game in major league history?

The earliest date for a regular-season major league game is March 25. On that date in 2008, the Red Sox defeated the Athletics 6-5 in 10 innings before 44,628 at the Tokyo Dome. The game started at 5:05 a.m. Boston time. The Sox scored a run in the ninth to tie the contest and two in the 10th before withstanding an Oakland rally in the bottom half. Daisuke Matsuzaka pitched five innings and allowed two runs and two hits. Brandon Moss homered and Manny Ramirez drove in two runs with two doubles. The Sox lost the second tilt of the two-game series in Japan 5-1 the following day. It was part of a trying road trip for the Red Sox. The club went to Japan from Florida for the series against the A's, arriving on March 20. Exhibition games in Los Angeles were followed by regular-season contests in Oakland on April 1 and 2 before three games in Toronto on April 4, 5 and 6. The Sox played their first 2008 game at Fenway Park on April 8.

# 18
## December

**T**he question of the day.
How did a David Ortiz jersey
become buried at the construction site of the new Yankee Stadium?

A construction worker's bid to
curse the New York Yankees by burying
a David Ortiz jersey in the new stadium
was foiled when the Yankees removed
the offending shirt from its burial spot. A
jackhammer was used to break though the
concrete on April 13, 2008, to pull the jersey out. The Yankees said
they learned that Gino Catignoli, a Red Sox fan on the construction crew, had buried the shirt in the stadium, scheduled to open
in 2009. The shirt was cleaned and put up for auction. It sold for
$175,000 with the proceeds going to charity.

# 19
## December

**T**he question of the day.
Who was Margo Adams?
Margo Adams was a 32-year-old woman from Costa Mesa, California, who sued Wade Boggs for $12 million dollars on June 3, 1988, claiming Boggs broke promises that he would support her during a four-year relationship. Boggs's attorney described Adams as "a groupie who feels somewhat rejected and in her obsession has tried to blackmail Mr. Boggs." Adams claimed she sacrificed her career as a mortgage broker to travel the country on 65 road trips with Boggs during an affair that began in 1984. Boggs later admitted that Adams was his companion on road trips, but denied there was an oral agreement that she would be compensated monetarily. The case created headlines for years. Boggs opened himself up to further ridicule by claiming he was addicted to sex during a television interview with Barbara Walters. Adams countered by posing nude in *Penthouse* and granted a two-part interview with the magazine published in April and May 1989. Boggs settled his palimony case with Adams out of court for an undisclosed amount on December 8, 1989.

**20**
December

**O**n this date in 2001, the Jean R. Yawkey Trust sold the Red Sox to a group headed by Marlins owner John Henry, former Padres owner Tom Werner, and former Orioles and Padres executive Larry Lucchino. Henry sold his stake in the Marlins to Jeffrey Loria, who owned the Expos. The Expos were subsequently operated by the other 29 clubs in major league baseball, a situation that existed until 2005 after the Expos moved to Washington and were renamed the Nationals. Major League Baseball formally recognized the transfer of the Red Sox to new ownership on January 16, 2002. The Henry group took control of the Sox on February 27. Before the sale was completed, Massachusetts Attorney General Thomas Reilly intervened. Reilly claimed the Red Sox rejected a larger offer, said to be $750 million, from a group headed by Miles Prentice. Reilly's responsibility was to ensure that the charities and charitable trusts standing to gain from liquidation of the Yawkey Trust's interests would receive maximum benefit from the sale. The Henry group and the limited partners then agreed to donate an additional $30 million over 10 years to youth and educational organizations.

# 21
## December

**T**he question of the day.
How many players started in right field on Opening Day for the Red Sox in the 12 seasons from 1988 through 1999?

There were 12 different starting right fielders for the Sox on Opening Day from 1988 through 1999. They were Mike Greenwell (1988), Dwight Evans (1989), Kevin Romine (1990), Tom Brunansky (1991), Phil Plantier (1992), Andre Dawson (1993), Billy Hatcher (1994), Mark Whiten (1995), Troy O'Leary (1996), Rudy Pemberton (1997), Darren Bragg (1998), and Trot Nixon (1999). Leaders in games started over the course of the season during those 12 years were Evans (1988 and 1989), Brunansky (1990, 1991 and 1992), Carlos Quintana (1993), Hatcher (1994), O'Leary (1995, 1996 and 1997), Bragg (1998) and Nixon (1999).

# 22 December

**T**he question of the day. How many officially recognized no-hitters have been thrown against the Red Sox?

The first officially recognized no-hitter of nine innings or more pitched against the Red Sox was by Bob Rhoades of the Indians on September 18, 1908, in Cleveland. Others have been tossed by Ed Walsh of the White Sox (August 27, 1911, in Chicago), George Mobridge of the Yankees (April 24, 1917, in Boston), Walter Johnson of the Senators (July 1, 1920, in Boston), Ted Lyons of the White Sox (August 21, 1926, in Boston), Bobby Burke of the Senators (August 8, 1931, in Washington), Allie Reynolds of the Yankees (September 28, 1951, in the first game of a double-header in New York), Jim Bunning of the Tigers (July 20, 1958, in the first game of a double-header in Boston), Tom Phoebus of the Orioles (April 27, 1968, in Baltimore), Dave Righetti of the Yankees (July 4, 1983, in New York) and Chris Bosio of the Mariners (April 22, 1993, in Seattle). In addition, Bobo Newsom of the Browns held the Sox hitless for the first 9⅔ innings on September 18, 1934, in St. Louis before Roy Johnson singled. The Red Sox won the game 2-1.

# 23
## December

**T**he question of the day.
What famous person did many of the Red Sox watch fall to his death?

Many of the Red Sox watched world-famous tightrope artist Karl Wallenda fall to his death in San Juan, Puerto Rico, on March 22, 1978. The Sox were in San Juan for a two-game series of exhibitions against the Pirates. Wallenda, who was 73-years-old, attempted to walk a 200-foot tightrope, 120 feet above the ground in a 30-mile-per-hour wind, at the Condaldo Holiday Inn. Wallenda lost his balance and fell to the street. He landed just 15 feet from where manager Don Zimmer was standing.

**B**

**24**
**December**

**O**n this date in 1967, Jim Lonborg suffered an injury to his left knee while skiing at the Heavenly Ski Resort in California near Lake Tahoe. Lonborg was coming off a season in which he was 22-9, pitched the American League pennant-clinching victory on the last day of the regular season, then won two World Series games against the Cardinals with a one-hitter and a three-hitter. Lonborg tore ligaments and completely misunderstood the severity of the injury. He struggled over the remainder of his years in Boston and became a constant reminder of what might have been. From 1968 through 1971, Lonborg was 27-29 with an ERA of 4.22. He never pitched more than 167⅔ innings in a season and spent parts of the 1970 and 1971 seasons in the minors. Lonborg was traded to the Brewers on October 11, 1971, and regained his effectiveness. In 1972 in Milwaukee, he was 14-12 with a 2.83 ERA while pitching for a losing team. The Brewers traded Lonborg to the Phillies, where he won 17 games in 1974 and 18 in 1976. After his playing career ended, Lonborg attended Tufts Dental School and became a dentist in Hanover, Massachusetts. On the Boston-based sitcom *Cheers,* a photo of lead character Sam Malone pitching for the Sox was on the wall of the set. It was actually of photo of Lonborg.

# 25

## December

**T**he question of the day. What was located at the present-day site of the Ruggles Street station 100 years ago?

Shuttle buses take Red Sox fans from the Ruggles Street station, part of the Orange line of the MBTA, to Fenway Park before and after each home game. Located at Ruggles Street and Columbus Avenue, many are unaware that the Ruggles Street station was the site of major league baseball from 1871 until 1914. It was used by the Boston Braves, a franchise now located in Atlanta. There were three different grandstands on the site, each known as South End Grounds. They were located on the north side of Columbus Avenue opposite the present day streets Cunard, Coventry and Burke. Most of the site is now occupied by the parking lot between Northeastern University's Columbus Parking Garage and the Ruggles Street station. The second edition of South End Grounds caught fire on May 16, 1894, and eventually spread throughout Roxbury, destroying 177 buildings. Huntington Grounds, home of the Red Sox from 1901 through 1911, was located just north of South End Grounds, on the other side of the tracks. The Braves abandoned South End Grounds in August 1914 and shared Fenway Park with the Red Sox until Braves Field opened on Commonwealth Avenue in August 1915.

**26**
**December**

**T**he question of the day?
Who was the first player to
hit two three-home-run games at
Fenway Park?

The first player to hit three or more
home runs in a game at Fenway Park
more than once was a visiting player.
Playing for the Indians, Joe Carter hit
three home runs and two singles to lead his
club to a 7-3 win over the Red Sox on August
29, 1986. He accomplished the feat again less than a year later during a 12-8 Boston win over Cleveland on May 28, 1987. The only
Red Sox batters with a pair of three-home-run games at Fenway are
Mo Vaughn in 1996 and 1997 and Nomar Garciaparra in 1999 and
2002.

# 27
## December

**T**he question of the day. Who was Lu Clinton? An outfielder with the Red Sox from 1960 through 1964, Lu Clinton was involved in a bizarre play on August 9, 1960, during a 5-3 loss to the Indians in Cleveland. Playing right field, Clinton kicked a fly ball hit by Vic Power over the fence. It happened when the game was tied 3-3 in the fifth inning with a Cleveland runner on base when Power hit a ball over Clinton's head. The ball hit the top of the wire fence and bounced toward Clinton, who was running with his back to the infield. The carom fell in front of Clinton and hit his foot while he was racing at full speed, causing him to accidentally kick it over the fence. Since the ball never touched the ground, umpire Al Smith ruled it a home run.

**B**

# 28
## December

**O**n this date in 1988, Wade Boggs was cut by two assailants in Gainesville, Florida. He was cut in the neck and threatened by one of the men at knifepoint. The inch-long wound was not serious enough to warrant medical attention. Police charged George Young, Jr., 23, with armed burglary and two counts of aggravated robbery. Edward Benjamin Cox, 31, was charged with aggravated assault and carrying a concealed weapon. Boggs said he was in his Jeep outside a Gainesville bar showing a handgun to two friends when two men blocked their vehicle. Young got out of the car carrying a knife and Cox waved a revolver at Boggs and his friends. Young jumped into the back seat of the Jeep and held a knife to Boggs's throat. In an interview with the press, Boggs said he used transcendental meditation to will himself invisible. Young was sentenced to 25 years in prison in July 1989.

# 29
## December

**T**he question of the day.
When did the Red Sox play 45 innings over three games in two days?

The Red Sox and White Sox were busy at the original Comiskey Park on July 12 and July 13, 1951, playing 45 innings over two days. On July 12, the Red Sox swept the White Sox 3-2 and 5-4 in a 26-inning twilight double-header. The second game was a 17-inning marathon. Clyde Vollmer drove in the winning run with a sacrifice fly. Ellis Kinder pitched the last 10 innings without allowing a run. Saul Rogovin pitched all 17 innings for Chicago. The day after playing 26 innings, the Red Sox and White Sox went 19 innings on July 13, with Chicago emerging with a 5-4 victory. The score was 2-2 after five innings before the two clubs combined for 13 consecutive scoreless frames. The Red Sox seemed to have the game in hand when they scored two runs in the top of the 19th, but the White Sox came back with three in their half off Harry Taylor and Ray Scarbourough for the victory. Mickey McDermott pitched the first 17 innings for the Red Sox. An outfielder, Vollmer had a surreal month in July, 1951. He began the month on the bench, but finished July with 13 homers and 40 RBIs. In August and September he turned back into a pumpkin, batting .218 with four homers in 206 at-bats.

**30**
**December**

**T**he question of the day.

How did the Red Sox' winning of the 2004 World Series change the ending of a movie?

The film *Fever Pitch* featured a diehard Red Sox fan played by Jimmy Fallon, who falls in love with a character played by Drew Barrymore, who fails to understand his devotion to the club. Directed by the Farrelly brothers, the screenplay, written by Lowell Ganz, was based on a novel by Nick Hornby. The original script assumed that the Red Sox would fail to win the World Series, as they had in every season since 1918. But the unexpected postseason run by the Sox changed those plans. At the end of the clinching fourth game in St. Louis, Fallon and Barrymore were allowed on the field to join in the celebration of Boston's first world championship in 86 years.

# 31
## December

**T**he question of the day.
When were Boston fans showered with scalding beans during a Red Sox game?

It never happened, although the story has been included in several highly respected books, among them *Diamonds: The Evolution of the Ballpark from Elysian Fields to Camden Yards* by Michael Gershman. According to the legend, on August 11, 1903, at Huntington Grounds, Rube Waddell of the Athletics hit a long foul ball that landed on the roof of the largest bean cannery in Boston. The ball jammed in the steam whistle causing a cauldron containing a ton of beans to explode. A shower of scalding beans descended on the bleachers and caused a small panic. The source was sportswriter Charles Dryden of the *Philadelphia North American* who wrote about the bizarre incident in the paper the following day. Subsequent research has revealed that Dryden made the whole thing up to amuse his readers. There were 10 newspapers in Boston in 1903, and none reported anything about an exploding cauldron of beans. In addition, there were no canneries located in the vicinity of Huntington Grounds.

**B**